THE
BLOOD

THE BLOOD

Its Power From Genesis to Jesus to You

FOREWORD BY JACK HAYFORD

BENNY HINN

CREATION
HOUSE
BOOKS ABOUT SPIRIT-LED LIVING
ORLANDO, FLORIDA

Creation House
Strang Communications Company
600 Rinehart Road
Lake Mary, FL 32746
Phone: (407) 333-3132
Fax: (407) 333-7100

Unless otherwise noted, all Scripture quotations are
from the New King James Version of the Bible.
Copyright © 1979, 1980, 1982 by Thomas
Nelson Inc., publishers. Used by permission.

Scripture quotations marked KJV are from
the King James Version of the Bible.

Scripture quotations marked NAS are from the
New American Standard Bible. Copyright © 1960, 1962, 1963,
1968, 1971, 1972, 1973, 1975, 1977 by
the Lockman Foundation. Used by permission.

Scripture quotations marked NIV are from the Holy
Bible, New International Version. Copyright © 1973, 1978, 1984,
International Bible Society. Used by permission.

Cloth:
First printing, October 1993
Second printing, December 1993
Third printing, December 1993
Fourth printing, January 1994

Paperback:
Second printing, November, 1994
Third printing, March 1995

This book is dedicated to
my wife, Suzanne,
who has been a precious,
wonderful partner to me since 1979.
She has stood with me,
praying for me and supporting me,
and the Lord has used her
to bless my life in a great way.

This book could not have been written
without the help of some good friends:
Stephen Strang, Neil Eskelin,
Deborah Poulalion, John Mason,
Dr. J. Rodman Williams, Dudley Hall,
Sheryl Palmquist, the staff at Creation House
and Strang Communications,
my co-workers at Orlando Christian Center
and so many others.
Thank you.

CONTENTS

*"Then Jesus, looking
at him, loved him."
Mark 10:21*

THE LAST THING I'm likely to do on vacation is watch a Christian telecast.

I'm a broadcaster myself, so tuning in to TV while I'm on vacation is anything but a change of pace. It was unusual, then, that I paused to watch anything, especially a Benny Hinn broadcast, since I'd never really taken the time to watch one before. That event is a very special memory to me now.

I had no idea what God was about to do in my

heart when I stopped "paging" with the TV remote and began noticing with a sense of gratitude the beauty of the worship taking place on Benny Hinn's program.

Benny has so many who love his ministry that it's a bit risky even to suggest I ever had any different impression of him. It can smack of criticism, professional jealousy or just plain unkindness. But I had never felt any of those things, nor did I ever stand opposed to Benny Hinn.

I simply had been busy with my own responsibilities and had no time for either 1) becoming more aware of his ministry or 2) being concerned with those who did criticize him. In short, I had no relationship with the man and no feelings, either positive or negative, about him.

Except for one.

I *did* feel that the little I'd seen and heard indicated that God's hand was on him, even though at times I was puzzled by his style — by the distracting practices I noted when paging by a telecast en route to something else.

But now I was watching.

As I observed the precious spirit of worship, I leaned back in my chair in the mountain cabin where my wife, Anna, and I were vacationing and began to enter into the praise that was wafting heavenward. Jesus was the center of attention. The name of Jesus was being magnificently glorified and adored. And as Benny led the service, I thought, "This man is an instrument in the hands of the Holy Spirit to bring people into the presence of God."

I'd never seen him lead others in worshipping Je-

12

sus, but as I did, something happened: God placed a distinct brotherly love for him in my heart. It was so pointed and so clearly an action of the Father in my soul that I later thought about Mark's words describing Jesus when the inquiring young man came to Him: "Then Jesus, looking at him, loved him."

Benny and I had met once, briefly, when he and his wife greeted me in a restaurant in Birmingham, England, where we each were speaking locally. But there was no way to suggest we had any real acquaintance.

Then suddenly, at this moment in the middle of my vacation, I knew God had given me a special sense of kinship with a man I hardly knew; in fact, one who more than anyone else I knew was often under criticism — though I was neither a foe nor in any personal way a friend. But right then, on that day, I "loved" the man with a heart full of gratitude to the God whose love often overflows our hearts by surprise.

It's interesting to look back on such moments — those times we all experience when the Holy Spirit is "up to" something but we have no idea what it is.

That's the way I view that summertime moment over a year ago. There was no way I could know then that within a very few weeks my telephone would ring and I'd be conversing with Benny Hinn for the first time.

It's for Benny himself to tell the details sometime of how God led him to contact a small number of leaders — most of whom knew him no better than I did — and ask for their counsel. I admired and commended him for doing this, not because I was one of those he trusted enough to ask counsel of; but I know of nothing more important for spiritual leaders to do than to submit themselves to one another.

To do so is not to substitute human counsel for Holy Spirit direction. It is wisely to acknowledge the facts of our humanness and our vulnerability to independent attitudes. It is those attitudes which open the door to the potential we all have for confusion, failure, error or lack of wisdom in how we serve in our personal callings.

"Brother Hayford," he said, "God is blessing my ministry in ways I could never imagine and could never produce. What is happening to me is something that I know He is doing, and I feel the need of brethren to whom I can turn and ask for input. We've all seen ministries fail for lack of accountability, and I don't want to be an embarrassment to the body of Christ. Would you be willing to let me come and spend time talking with you about God's ways and God's work?"

Even while he was speaking I knew why the Holy Spirit had prompted my heart those few days before. As we conversed, I expressed my friendly availability — "Benny, God's hand is on you to bring people into His presence. I'll be glad to do anything I can to help you keep your ministry focussed so that people are aware of Jesus more than of you, because I believe that's what you really want."

During the year since that time, Benny Hinn has testified to his desire to renew his focus on the essentials of the truth of God's Word in his ministry and to remove anything that would distract from his priority: to glorify Jesus Christ alone, our loving and mighty Savior.

Hosts of leaders like me are confirming this assertive effort on the part of a God-graced messenger to *be* what he is called to be. Praise God for the Christ-like humility which is, I believe, opening the door to a vastly broadened ministry of Jesus' life and power through a vessel named Benny.

This book is one of the hallmarks of this new time in his life. It is not only a pointed focus on the ultimate foundational essential in the gospel, but it is also a fresh, Spirit-anointed truth to which I believe He — the Holy Spirit — is seeking to alert all God's people at this time.

Only days before Benny Hinn invited me to write this foreword, I had experienced a very special heart-stirring concerning the blood of Jesus. So profound was the quickening that I had set aside time for study and made plans to bring a series on this subject to my flock at The Church on the Way.

Discovering the plans for this book deepened my conviction: *The blood of Jesus is a primary theme the Holy Spirit has for the church today.*

Why? First, *all power* which flows to mankind with redeeming grace and glory flows because of the blood of Jesus. Second, *no confusion* about the Savior's person or work can abide in an atmosphere where the blood and the cross are taught in the light of God's Word. And, third, *no power of hell* can withstand the proclamation of the blood of Jesus, whether it is declared from a pulpit or spoken over a home or a heart.

I'm grateful that this book has been written. It is a testimony to the greatest truth known to mankind: that the Son of God has declared, "It is finished," and that through His blood and cross *alone,* He has broken the power of sin, death and hell. He is the Lord!

It is also a testimony of a man's answer to God's call to focus on priorities that will point every listener, viewer or reader to Jesus — and bring them into the presence of God.

Glory to the Lamb that was slain!

Jack W. Hayford, pastor
The Church on the Way
Van Nuys, California
September 1993

The reason I am writing
this book is summed up in the words
of R. A. Torrey:

*"We must know the power
of the blood if we are to know
the power of God.
Our knowing experimentally
the power of the Word,
the power of the Holy Spirit,
and the power of prayer,
is dependent upon
our knowing the power
of the blood of Christ."*[1]

ONE————————————————————

POWER AND PROMISE

BEING RAISED IN Israel has given me a deep appreciation and respect for the Jewish people. Because of their history, they have an emotional link to their land that is beyond description. Countless Jews also continue Old Testament practices even to this day.

My family, however, was not Jewish. My mother, Clemence, was of Armenian descent. And my father, Constandi, came from a family that had immigrated from Greece to Egypt and then to Palestine. To add to my multicultural childhood, I was christened in the Greek Orthodox church, spoke French at school, Arabic in our home and Hebrew outside the home.

Immediately after Israel's Six Day War of 1967, my father gathered our family of eight children together and announced that we would be emigrating to another country. The next year we arrived in Toronto, Canada, with just a few earthly possessions. I was sixteen years old.

Then in 1972 my life was totally transformed by an encounter with Christ at a morning prayer meeting conducted by students at the school I attended. At home after school I opened the pages of a big black Bible that had not been used for years. After reading from the Gospels nonstop for several hours, I found myself saying out loud, "Jesus, come into my heart."

I thank God He did.

Later that week I went with my newly found Christian friends to their church. The people who attended were an exuberant throng of Christians who met every Thursday in St. Paul's Cathedral, an Anglican church in downtown Toronto.

I had never heard people speak so openly about the blood of Christ. They would sing, "Oh, the blood of Jesus!" They would pray, "Lord, cover us with Your blood."

If you have read my book *Good Morning, Holy Spirit*, you know what happened when I had a personal encounter with the Holy Spirit just before Christmas in 1973. It totally transformed my life. And from that moment the Bible took on a whole new dimension. Day after day I became absorbed in Scripture, and the Holy Spirit became my friend and guide.

I was like a thirsty sponge as I began to learn about everything from original sin to the marriage supper of the Lamb. And what I didn't understand, I asked the Holy Spirit to reveal. That was when I realized that God's relationship to man was held together by a blood covenant.

Days of Discovery

During those exciting days as a young Christian, I was attending a church on Sundays pastored by Maxwell Whyte. He was an outstanding teacher of God's Word who became a spiritual mentor to me. Pastor Whyte was the minister who baptized me in water.

One of his constant themes was the blood of Christ. His accounts of the outpouring of the Holy Spirit at the turn of the century will never be erased from my memory. He told the story of the mighty move of the Holy Spirit that came to Kilsyth, Scotland, in 1908. Pastor Whyte said that the visitation came spontaneously as a result of recognizing the power of the blood of Jesus. He said, "A brother named John Ried, sitting in the midst of the prayer group, suddenly raised his hands and said, 'The blood of Jesus.' "

Immediately the Holy Spirit descended on the gathering, and people began to receive the Pentecostal experience all over the room. The revival spread throughout England.[1]

In his book *The Power of the Blood*, Pastor Whyte tells of living in England during World War II.

We went through many dangerous air raids when buzz bombs were flying everywhere. But we were able to lie down with our children and sleep through much of it. The protection of the Blood of Jesus was so real that it seemed like we were sleeping in a strong shelter. In fact, we used to speak of the Blood as the "best air raid shelter in the world."[2]

Pastor Whyte said that every night before they went to sleep they would ask the Lord to cover them, their home and their children with the blood. One night thirteen bombs landed within three quarters of a mile from their home. Aside from some minor damage to the house, they were all kept safe.

I remember his telling our congregation again and again, "I have never known the active, audible pleading of the blood to fail."

Because of his ministry, my interest in the power of the blood of Christ grew and multiplied. And I began to study it for myself to see what the Word really said.

He Gave His Life

Many years later, after I became the pastor of Orlando Christian Center in Florida, God gave me an understanding of the blood covenant that would forever change my life and ministry.

One Saturday afternoon I had stayed home to study the Scriptures about the blood covenant so I could teach it to my congregation. I was sitting outside in the backyard of my home studying and praying. "Lord, give me an understanding of the blood," I asked. The second I said that I felt the presence of the Lord and began to weep.

That day the blood of Christ took on a whole new meaning. The Holy Spirit began showing me that the blood of Jesus represents His life. I realized more than ever that when Christ shed His blood at Calvary, He gave us His very *life*. And when we ask the Lord to wash us and cover us with His blood, we will experience His life-giving power.

Throughout my ministry I have seen that Christians have a limited knowledge of the atonement. As a result, they have not experienced the freedom God has for their lives.

For example, many believers tell me that satan continues to oppress them. It comes as a surprise when I tell them I have not experienced any demonic oppression on me since I began asking God to cover me with the blood.

Before that I was depressed at times and felt that my mind was blocked. Sometimes when I prayed I felt a horrible oppression come upon me. I had nightmares and sometimes felt that something was literally choking me.

But when God gave me that enormous understanding of the blood, and I began to ask for a blood covering through prayer, that "thing" was completely broken. Years have passed since I have had that kind of attack.

There is power in the blood of Jesus. There is no question about it.

But at the same time, the blood does not have

"magical" power by itself. The power comes from the Lord Jesus Himself, and He is the one who will act on your behalf when you apply His blood through prayer.

We apply Jesus' blood through prayer and faith. But it is the Lord who covers us; we do not cover ourselves.

Why have I written this book?

- To open your eyes to the importance God places on the topic of the blood covenant.

- To demonstrate the power of the blood of Jesus.

- To show how you and I can come into God's presence through the blood of His Son.

- To help you understand the "great" grace that God bestows on us because of the blood of Jesus.

- To lead you to a greater freedom in Christ than you have ever experienced.

This is a book I want you to read with your Bible open. If God places such an emphasis on the blood from Genesis to Revelation, there is a message in His Word for you.

The Completed Picture

When I asked the Holy Spirit to give me an understanding of the blood covenant, I had dozens of questions. But He gave me the answers from the Word, and I want to share them with you.

- What does the Scripture mean in Hebrews 12:24 when it says that the blood "speaks better things than that of Abel"?

- Why was the leper sprinkled with blood seven times (Lev. 14:7)?

- How can the blood of Jesus be applied in our lives today?

- How is God's grace connected to the blood of His Son?

- How can the blood of Christ provide protection for your household?

- What does the Scripture teach about the blood of the cross and the anointing?

- What does Hebrews 9:12 mean when it says, "With His own blood He entered the Most Holy Place once for all, having obtained eternal redemption"?

- How can we use the blood of Jesus to defeat the enemy in our lives?

I pray that as you continue reading and understanding the blood covenant, you will experience God's wonderful presence.

TWO

FROM THE
BEGINNING

OUR HOME IN Jaffa, Israel, seemed much larger than it was. To save land the building was designed for three families, with a separate home on each level.

On the top floor lived Mr. Hanna and his family. He was a Lebanese who was married to a Jewish woman from Hungary. But Mr. Hanna was more than a neighbor. Because of the bond that was established between my father and him, he became a second father to the eight children in our family.

Mr. Hanna and my father, Constandi, entered into a pact that will never be erased from my memory. Using a razor-sharp blade, each man made an incision on his wrist until blood seeped to the surface. Then they placed their wrists tightly together and allowed the blood to mingle.

On the table before them were two glasses of wine. My dad held his wrist over one of the goblets and let several drops of blood fall into it. Mr. Hanna did the same.

Next, they mixed the wine together, and each drank from the other man's cup. At that moment they became blood brothers. In the Eastern culture and among many other people of the world, it is the strongest bond that can be made between two men.

For this kind of covenant, some Easterners will also sign a written agreement that says, "If you are unable to provide for your children, I will become a father to them and sustain them. If you become ill or die, I will be responsible for the well-being of your family."

It is more than a legal pact. It is a vow that is sealed in blood and will never be broken.

When our family emigrated from Israel to Canada and I became a Christian, the Holy Spirit began to reveal God's Word to me. I had seen the influence of the blood pact in the Eastern culture. Then the Holy Spirit showed me how much more powerful God's blood covenant is. From Genesis to Revelation there is a crimson stream that is the life-giving source of power, protection and promise for you and for me today.

The Breath of Life

The story of creation itself marks the beginning of the role of the blood covenant in God's plan for humanity.

Our creation was a three-step process.

First, "the Lord God formed man of the dust of the ground" (Gen. 2:7). I can almost see Him scooping some mud into His hand and literally squeezing it into shape. At that same time, I believe God created our blood.

Second, God "breathed into his nostrils the breath of life" (Gen. 2:7). At this point, I believe our spirits came into being. The Scriptures often represent God's Spirit as His breath. So I believe God as a Spirit created our spirits.

Third, "man became a living soul," (Gen. 2:7, KJV). After man received his body and spirit, then he was a distinct individual (or a soul).

The spirit, body and soul that God created have a distinct function.

- The *spirit* within us is the part that knows God intimately. It is God-conscious.

- Our *body* is the shell we dwell in. It is world-conscious.

- The *soul* is our intellect, will and emotion. It is self-conscious.

Like an archaeologist unearthing a hidden treasure, I was jubilant as I studied the Word of God and realized the distinct parts God created. My spirit is the part of me that communes with God; my physical being is what is in contact with the earthly things of this world; and my soul is the part that feels, understands, thinks and decides.

I believe another amazing thing occurred at creation. Leviticus records, "The life of the flesh is in the blood" (17:11). Therefore, when God breathed the breath of life into Adam, I believe his blood was enlivened.

For centuries, medical science has studied the powerful functions of blood. They know it carries oxygen and food through our bodies by circulating through our veins and arteries. It also acts as a defense against infection. But there is much that they *don't* know about the importance God places on the blood.

Chaos in the Garden

As we begin to comprehend the tremendous power of the blood covenant, it is important to recall what happened in the garden of Eden. When God created Adam, he was a perfect being. He had a magnificent mind that was able to name every animal and remember their names.

At that time, the first man and woman lived in perfect harmony with God. He walked with them in the cool of the day. They had fellowship, and they knew God intimately.

But an enemy was lurking in the garden.

Now the serpent was more cunning than any beast of the field which the Lord God had made. And he said to the woman, "Has God indeed said, 'You shall not eat of every tree of the garden'?" (Gen. 3:1).

Satan was cunning and sly. He came to the woman with a question about God's instructions regarding eating from the tree. He asked her, "Has God indeed said, 'You shall not eat of every tree of the garden'?" (Gen. 3:1).

The devil wields this weapon of words because he wants us to question God — His faithfulness, His love, His promises and His power. He was questioning the woman: "Did God really say that?" Her answer shows she believed the tempter rather than what God said. And she disobeyed.

The woman replied to the serpent, "We may eat the fruit of the trees of the garden; but of the fruit of the tree which is in the midst of the garden, God has said, 'You shall not eat it, nor shall you touch it, *lest you die*' " (Gen. 3:2-3, italics added).

Eve only said, "...lest you die," but the Lord said, "You shall *surely* die" (Gen. 2:17, italics added).

Then satan lied to the woman and said, "You will not surely die. For God knows that in the day you eat of it your eyes will be opened, and you will be like God, knowing good and evil" (Gen. 3:4-5).

It has always been satan's desire to be like God. Scripture records that he said in his heart, "I will ascend into heaven, I will exalt my throne above the stars of God" (Is. 14:13).

Satan had been banished from heaven for trying to be like God. Now he was attempting to offer the same promise of god-like status to the first woman. And he has not stopped. Thousands of years later, he is still planting the same thoughts into unsuspecting hearts.

The Flesh and the Devil

The first woman not only fell for the lie, but she also enticed Adam to join her, and original sin entered the heart of man.

> And when the woman saw that the tree was good for food, and that it was pleasant to the eyes, and a tree to be desired to make one wise, she took of the fruit thereof, and did eat, and gave also unto her husband with her; and he did eat (Gen. 3:6, KJV).

In that one Scripture verse we find three great temptations satan uses:

1. The lust of the flesh. (The tree was good for food.)

2. The lust of the eyes. (It was pleasant to look at.)

3. The pride of life. (The tree offered wisdom.)

Why does the enemy bring these forms of temptation against us? His deadly design is to pull us into a sinful world. But we are warned:

> Do not love the world or the things in the world. If anyone loves the world, the love of

the Father is not in him. For all that is in the world — the lust of the flesh, the lust of the eyes, and the pride of life — is not of the Father but is of the world (1 John 2:15-16).

Satan tried the same three temptations during his encounter with Jesus in the desert. He said, "If You are the Son of God, command that these stones become bread" (Matt. 4:3). What was he offering? The lust of the flesh.

When "the devil took Him up on an exceedingly high mountain, and showed Him all the kingdoms of the world and their glory" (Matt. 4:8), he tempted Christ with the lust of the eyes.

And he appealed to the pride of life by saying to the Lord:

If You are the Son of God, throw Yourself down. For it is written:

"He shall give His angels charge
over you,"

and,

"In their hands they shall bear you
up,
Lest you dash your foot against a
stone" (Matt. 4:6).

Even satan knew the Word. He told Jesus, "It is written," and quoted Psalm 91:11-12.

But Jesus knew the Word even better. With the authority of heaven He said, "It is written, 'You shall not tempt the Lord your God' " (Matt. 4:7). Three separate times He said, "It is written" (Matt. 4:4,7,10). Jesus finally said:

> Away with you, Satan! For it is written, "You shall worship the Lord your God, and Him only you shall serve" (Matt. 4:10).

The enemy is still using the same tactics today. But the Lord Jesus defeated satan with the power of the Word, and the same power is available to us today.

God's Word is a powerful weapon against the enemy's attacks because it reveals to us the conditions and promises of God's blood covenant. From the moment of the original sin, God introduced the blood covenant as a means of covering, or atonement. Here is how it happened.

THREE

THE COVERING

WHEN ADAM AND his wife yielded to the snare of satan, "the eyes of both of them were opened, and they knew that they were naked; and they sewed fig leaves together and made themselves coverings" (Gen. 3:7). The fact that they even tried to make clothes for themselves showed that they realized their need for a covering.

The instant they yielded to temptation they lost God's consciousness and gained self-consciousness.

They lost sight of God and His glory.

I am fully convinced that before the fall the first man and woman did not see their physical nakedness as shameful. They may have been without the clothing that you and I wear, but I believe they were covered with the glory of God.

Because they were accustomed to being blanketed by God, after they sinned they made themselves a covering (Gen. 3:7). When they first gained sight of self, they realized how empty and exposed they truly were and even "hid themselves from the presence of the Lord God among the trees of the garden" (Gen. 3:8).

The Scriptures declare later that they heard the voice of God walking in the garden in the cool of the day saying, "Where are you?" (Gen. 3:8-9).

And Adam answered, "I heard Your voice in the garden, and I was afraid because I was naked; and I hid myself" (Gen. 3:9-10).

God wanted to know, "Who told you that you were naked? Have you eaten from the tree of which I commanded you that you should not eat?" (Gen. 3:11).

Adam blamed his wife. When God asked the woman, she blamed the devil. "The serpent deceived me, and I ate" (Gen. 3:13).

Curses and Judgments

Because of their sin, God pronounced five separate curses and judgments.

> 1. God cursed the serpent. "So the Lord God said to the serpent: 'Because you

have done this, you are cursed more than all cattle, and more than every beast of the field; on your belly you shall go, and you shall eat dust all the days of your life" (Gen. 3:14).

2. God pronounced judgment on Eve. "I will greatly multiply your sorrow and your conception; in pain you shall bring forth children" (Gen. 3:16).

3. The Lord judged Adam to a life of toil. "Because you have heeded the voice of your wife, and have eaten from the tree of which I commanded you, saying, 'You shall not eat of it': Cursed is the ground for your sake; in toil you shall eat of it all the days of your life" (Gen. 3:17).

4. God cursed the ground (Gen. 3:17). "Both thorns and thistles it shall bring forth for you" (Gen. 3:18).

5. Then the Lord sentenced Adam to eventual death. "In the sweat of your face you shall eat bread till you return to the ground, for out of it you were taken; for dust you are, and to dust you shall return" (Gen. 3:19).

In the midst of God's judgment, however, is a wonderful promise of redemption. The Lord said to the serpent:

> I will put enmity
> Between you and the woman,
> And between your seed and her Seed;
> He shall bruise your head,
> And you shall bruise His heel (Gen. 3:15).

The Lord declared that He was going to send the seed of the woman to bring deliverance. It was a promise fulfilled in the conquest of Christ on the cross over satan. And that is a victory in which every believer shares.

The First Sacrifice

Now when all of these events took place, God did something marvelous. He initiated the first blood sacrifice.

> Unto Adam also and to his wife did the Lord
> God make coats of skins, and clothed them
> (Gen. 3:21, KJV).

We need to remember that Adam and Eve had run from the presence of God and had lost His glory. They were naked and ashamed, attempting to cover themselves with leaves.

That is when God selected some animals, perhaps lambs, and killed them.[1] He covered the man and woman with the skins (Gen. 3:21). I believe that the animals had just been slain and that the skins were still moist with blood when God used them to cover Adam and Eve.

Please note: God's first sacrifice covered Adam and

Eve's sin with animals' blood. As we will see, His final sacrifice covered you and me with the blood of His only begotten Son. When the Bible says, "It is the blood that makes atonement for the soul" (Lev. 17:11), the word *atonement* means "to cover." That is why I believe the shedding of blood had to be a part of the covering. When Adam and Eve sinned, they lost their close communion with God. But through the blood covenant, God was declaring that their sins were atoned for. The blood one day would bring back the fellowship and joy.

From the time of Adam to the time of Christ, Scripture is filled with accounts of how God entered into blood covenants with His people.

- Noah's first act after coming out of the ark was to make a blood covenant with the Lord. He "built an altar to the Lord, and took of every clean animal and of every clean bird, and offered burnt offerings on the altar" (Gen. 8:20).

- Abraham was told by the Lord: "This is My covenant which you shall keep, between Me and you and your descendants after you: Every male child among you shall be circumcised" (Gen. 17:10).

- Moses, after God delivered the commandments, gathered the people together and offered young bulls as a sacrifice. "And Moses took the blood, sprinkled it on the people, and said, 'This is the blood of the covenant which the Lord has made with you according to all these words' " (Ex. 24:8).

- Abraham and Abimelech sealed their relationship by covenant and the setting apart of seven ewe lambs (Gen. 21:22-32).

- The covenant between Jacob and Laban was sealed when "Jacob offered a sacrifice on the mountain, and called his brethren to eat bread. And they ate bread and stayed all night on the mountain" (Gen. 31:54).

Thousands of people have entered into a blood covenant like the one my father and Mr. Hanna made. In the Old Testament it was common for men to "cut a covenant" and make a pact through the shedding of blood.

Accounts of blood covenants are not only found in Scripture, but in history. It is still practiced by many tribes in Africa and societies in Asia, South America and the Middle East.

The pact-until-death is entered into for a variety of reasons, from joining into a business partnership to protecting a weaker tribe from a stronger one. In many instances it has turned bitter enemies into life-long friends.

Stanley and the Chieftain

Henry Stanley was a journalist in the 1870s who traveled through the jungles of Africa in search of the famed missionary David Livingstone.

On numerous occasions Stanley observed the rite of blood-brotherhood, or "strong friendship," to protect himself in his travels. Once he made a compact with Mirambo, the warrior chief of Western Unyamwezi.

Stanley first encountered the warrior chief when his expedition was defeated by Mirambo's forces during his initial search for Livingstone in 1871. He compared the chief's leadership in warfare to Napoleon and Frederick the Great.

During his second exploring expedition Stanley hoped for a while to avoid Mirambo. But he became impressed by his powers and decided to meet him. He wanted to make strong friendship with him.

They met, and Stanley was quite taken with the warrior chief. The African hero and the heroic American agreed to make strong friendship with each other.

Stanley's "chief captain," Manwa Sera, was asked to seal the friendship of the two men by performing the ceremony of blood-brotherhood between them.

Mirambo and Stanley sat facing each other on a straw carpet. Sera made an incision in each of their right legs, from which he extracted blood, and interchanged it. He then exclaimed aloud:

> If either of you break this brotherhood now established between you, may the lion devour him, the serpent poison him, bitterness be in his food, his friends desert him, his gun burst in his hands and wound him, and everything that is bad do wrong to him until death.

At the end of the covenant, they gave a gift to each other in the usual ratification of the compact.

The same blood flowed in both Stanley's and Mirambo's veins. They were brothers and friends in a sacred covenant — life for life.[2]

Now this was a pagan ritual and is in no way endorsed by Scripture. But let's look at the Bible and see the way God used blood in covenants with His people.

FOUR

An Eternal Covenant

I HAVE ALWAYS been fascinated with the story of Cain and Abel, the first two sons of Adam and Eve. They may have been twins. The Bible says that Eve conceived once and delivered twice.

> Now Adam knew Eve his wife, and she conceived and bore Cain, and said, "I have acquired a man from the Lord." Then she bore again, this time his brother Abel (Gen. 4:1-2).

They may have looked alike, but they chose two different occupations.

> Now Abel was a keeper of sheep, but Cain was a tiller of the ground (Gen. 4:2).

After what their parents had experienced, it was only natural that the children were taught the principle of presenting gifts to the Lord.

> And in the process of time it came to pass that Cain brought an offering of the fruit of the ground to the Lord. Abel also brought of the firstborn of his flock and of their fat (Gen. 4:3-4).

Scripture records that "the Lord respected Abel and his offering, but He did not respect Cain and his offering" (Gen. 4:4-5). What was the difference? Why did God accept one offering and reject the other?

The answer is found in Hebrews 11:4.

> By faith Abel offered to God a more excellent sacrifice than Cain, through which he obtained witness that he was righteous, God testifying of his gifts; and through it he being dead still speaks.

It was "by faith" that Abel offered a blood sacrifice to the Lord. We know that "faith comes by hearing" (Rom. 10:17), so it's reasonable to assume the two sons knew the power of the blood because their parents shared their experience in the garden.

How did Abel know to offer a blood sacrifice? I believe Adam and Eve told their sons what God expected. I believe God gave a revelation of the blood covenant to the first man and woman when He sacrificed animals to atone for their sin and clothed them with skins that may have been wet with blood (Gen. 3:21). It was a sign of the redemption and deliverance that was to come. No doubt Eve wondered, "Which one of my sons will bruise the serpent's head?" (Gen. 3:15).

Both sons knew that God demanded a blood covenant. That is why God asked Cain, "Why are you angry? Why is your face downcast? If you do what is right, will you not be accepted?" (Gen. 4:6-7, NIV). Cain knew what was right, but he didn't do it. Instead he offered a gift of vegetation, and God refused it.

Abel, however, was obedient to the Lord. By faith he offered an animal sacrifice — the "firstfruits" of his flock. The substitute blood was given by Abel from a heart of love and trust. He was reaching out to be in covenant with the Lord.

Cain offered a gift, but it was not what God required. There is a great difference between presenting what the Lord demands and merely giving a present.

> Has the Lord as great delight in burnt offerings and sacrifices,
> As in obeying the voice of the Lord?
> Behold, to obey is better than sacrifice (1 Sam. 15:22).

An Unthinkable Act

What was Cain's reaction to God's disapproval?

> So Cain was very angry, and his face was downcast.
> Then the Lord said to Cain, "Why are you angry? Why is your face downcast? If you do what is right, will you not be accepted? But if you do not do what is right, sin is crouching at your door; it desires to have you, but you must master it" (Gen. 4:5-7, NIV).

Here's what God was telling the disobedient son: "The choice is yours. You can make the decision to choose between right or wrong." It is a message that permeates Scripture. We have power over sin if we walk in faith and obedience to God.

But Cain ignored God's warning, and his next step was to commit an act that was unthinkable.

> Now Cain said to his brother Abel, "Let's go out to the field." And while they were in the field, Cain attacked his brother Abel and killed him (Gen. 4:8, NIV).

The first murder in the Bible was committed with deliberate deceit. Cain called his unsuspecting brother out to a field and took his life. The killing was also the result of spiritual disobedience. He rebelled against presenting a blood covenant to the Lord.

What a contrast! The Word tells us that we "should love one another, not as Cain who was of the wicked

44

one and murdered his brother. And why did he murder him? Because his works were evil and his brother's righteous" (1 John 3:11-12).

Immediately after the tragic event, the Lord asked Cain, "Where is Abel your brother?" And he said, "I do not know. Am I my brother's keeper?" (Gen. 4:9).

As my good friend Carlton Pearson of Tulsa, Oklahoma, says: "If you aren't your brother's keeper, you are your brother's killer."

Cain's answer was more than an outright lie. It was a statement of indifference, even contempt.

Once again God spoke to Cain and asked, "What have you done? The voice of your brother's blood cries out to Me from the ground" (Gen. 4:10).

Abel's blood cried out for justice to be done. The blood of Jesus, speaking better things, cries out that justice has been done and our sins have been forgiven. Abel's blood cried out for vengeance; the blood of Jesus pleads for forgiveness and restoration.

As Christians we have come "to Jesus the Mediator of the new covenant, and to the blood of sprinkling that speaks better things than that of Abel" (Heb. 12:24).

Because of his sin, Cain would never know God's blessing. The Lord proclaimed this judgment:

> So now you are cursed from the earth, which has opened its mouth to receive your brother's blood from your hand. When you till the ground, it shall no longer yield its strength to you. A fugitive and a vagabond you shall be on the earth (Gen. 4:11-12).

My friend, don't reject the message of the blood. It isn't worth the risk. Cain's punishment was for more than the murder of his brother. It was also because he disobeyed a revelation of God's blood covenant. Those who refuse God's covenant are in jeopardy of becoming hopeless wanderers, eternally lost.

The Bible makes it clear that if we reject Christ's blood, we have offended God's Holy Spirit.

> Anyone who has rejected Moses' law dies without mercy on the testimony of two or three witnesses. Of how much worse punishment, do you suppose, will he be thought worthy who has trampled the Son of God underfoot, counted the blood of the covenant by which he was sanctified a common thing, and insulted the Spirit of grace? (Heb. 10:28-29).

The blood is not a topic to be shunned, ignored or rebuffed. It is still our vital link to God.

The Promise

One great blood covenant established in the Old Testament is called the Abrahamic covenant.

> The Lord appeared to Abram and said to him, "I am Almighty God; walk before Me and be blameless. And I will make My covenant between Me and you, and will multiply you exceedingly" (Gen. 17:1-2).

Abraham "fell on his face, and God talked with him, saying: 'As for Me, behold, My covenant is with you, and you shall be a father of many nations' " (Gen. 17:3-4).

God knew that His servant was about to become a transformed man, and He even changed his name.

> No longer shall your name be called Abram, but your name shall be Abraham; for I have made you a father of many nations (Gen. 17:5).

Abraham was given a new name by God, and he became a different man. Abraham's relationship to the Lord also changed so much that the Lord would now be called the "God of Abraham." A blood covenant with God transforms lives.

Then God told Abraham:

> I will make you exceedingly fruitful; and I will make nations of you, and kings shall come from you. And I will establish My covenant between Me and you and your descendants after you in their generations, for an everlasting covenant, to be God to you and your descendants after you (Gen. 17:6-7).

The Lord also promised to give Abraham and his descendants "the land of Canaan, as an everlasting possession" if they would keep the covenant (Gen. 17:8-9).

Most important, this covenant would be marked by the shedding of blood.

> This is My covenant which you shall keep,
> between Me and you and your descendants
> after you: Every male child among you shall
> be circumcised; and you shall be circumcised
> in the flesh of your foreskins, and it shall be
> a sign of the covenant between Me and you
> (Gen. 17:10-11).

What was the sign of the Abrahamic covenant? Circumcision. Every male child was to have this rite performed when he was eight days old. As a result he would not only enter into the covenant, but take part in God's promises to Abraham.

God honored the covenant so that, even at his advanced age, Abraham was able to father a child. His wife, Sarah, who was ninety, conceived and bore a son. They named him Isaac.

The Ultimate Test

After Isaac was born, God chose to test Abraham's faith in the covenant promise to make him the father of a great nation.

> Now it came to pass after these things that
> God tested Abraham, and said to him, "Abraham!"
>
> And he said, "Here I am."
>
> Then He said, "Take now your son, your
> only son Isaac, whom you love, and go to
> the land of Moriah, and offer him there as a
> burnt offering on one of the mountains of
> which I shall tell you" (Gen. 22:1-2).

The Lord was giving Abraham the ultimate test. When satan tempts us, he wants to provoke us to evil. But when God tests us, He seeks to reinforce, strengthen and fortify our commitment. Remember the difference: God *tests* us. Satan *tempts* us.

There was no question that Abraham's true affections were about to be exposed. Whom did he love more? Isaac or God? After all, the child had been given as a miracle. Would he love the gift more than the Giver? The Bible says:

> Abraham rose early in the morning and saddled his donkey, and took two of his young men with him, and Isaac his son; and he split the wood for the burnt offering, and arose and went to the place of which God had told him. Then on the third day Abraham lifted his eyes and saw the place afar off. And Abraham said to his young men, "Stay here with the donkey; the lad and I will go yonder and worship, and we will come back to you" (Gen. 22:3-5).

How could Abraham declare, "We will come back"? He had total faith in God, for God had promised: "In Isaac your seed shall be called" (Gen. 21:12). He believed that "God was able to raise him up, even from the dead" (Heb. 11:19).

That was great faith in God from a man who had no idea what was going to happen on that mountain.

As a father of four children, my heart is touched when I read the account of their conversation.

So Abraham took the wood of the burnt offering and laid it on Isaac his son; and he took the fire in his hand, and a knife, and the two of them went together. But Isaac spoke to Abraham his father and said, "My father!"

And he said, "Here I am, my son."

Then he said, "Look, the fire and the wood, but where is the lamb for a burnt offering?"

And Abraham said, "My son, God will provide for Himself the lamb for a burnt offering." So the two of them went together (Gen. 22:6-8).

When they reached the appointed place, Abraham built an altar and placed the wood in order. Isaac must have been filled with faith, too. The Scriptures do not mention any resistance when Abraham "bound Isaac his son and laid him on the altar, upon the wood" (Gen. 22:9).

I can only imagine the emotions each of them felt when Abraham "stretched out his hand and took the knife to slay his son" (Gen. 22:10).

But the Angel of the Lord called to him from heaven and said, "Abraham, Abraham!"

So he said, "Here I am."

And He said, "Do not lay your hand on the lad, or do anything to him; for now I know that you fear God, since you have not withheld your son, your only son, from Me" (Gen. 22:11-12).

Abraham had passed God's test. He chose the Giver over the gift. But the offering of blood still had to be presented.

> Then Abraham lifted his eyes and looked, and there behind him was a ram caught in a thicket by its horns. So Abraham went and took the ram, and offered it up for a burnt offering instead of his son (Gen. 22:13).

When we demonstrate our faith in God by our obedience, He not only *promises* to provide for us — He *will* provide!

Then the Angel of the Lord called to Abraham a second time and said:

> Because you have done this thing, and have not withheld your son, your only son — blessing I will bless you, and multiplying I will multiply your descendants as the stars of the heaven and as the sand which is on the seashore; and your descendants shall possess the gate of their enemies (Gen. 22:16-17).

Because of Abraham's faith and obedience, God fulfilled His promise to make him the father of a great nation.

The Exodus

While I was studying the blood covenant many years ago the Lord showed me something very exciting. It was because of the Abrahamic covenant that God brought Israel out of Egypt.

> Now it happened in the process of time that the king of Egypt died. Then the children of Israel groaned because of the bondage, and they cried out; and their cry came up to God because of the bondage. So God heard their groaning, and God remembered His covenant with Abraham, with Isaac, and with Jacob (Ex. 2:23-24).

Moses, before leading the great exodus, learned that God would punish those who did not keep the covenant. Evidently Moses failed to have one of his two sons circumcised. During a journey from his father-in-law's house back to Egypt, "it came to pass on the way, at the encampment, that the Lord met him and sought to kill him" (Ex. 4:24). The text is not clear whether God sought to destroy Moses or the son. But it is clear that Moses' wife, Zipporah, knew what caused God's wrath. She "took a sharp stone and cut off the foreskin of her son and cast it at Moses' feet...So He let him go" (Ex. 4:25-26).

It was a lesson the great leader would never forget. God will not honor a man who has broken His covenant.

As Moses led the children of Israel into the desert, the covenant was the binding force that held the great throng of people together. The Ten Commandments were much more than rules to live by. They became known as the law of the covenant.

Try to imagine what it must have been like when

Moses came down from Mount Sinai to the nearly two million waiting Israelites.

Moses told the people what God had declared, and they "answered with one voice and said, 'All the words which the Lord has said we will do' " (Ex. 24:3). It was an important step toward a new blood covenant between God and His people.

Early the next morning Moses built an altar at the foot of the mountain.

> Then he sent young men of the children of Israel, who offered burnt offerings and sacrificed peace offerings of oxen to the Lord. And Moses took half the blood and put it in basins, and half the blood he sprinkled on the altar. Then he took the Book of the Covenant and read in the hearing of the people. And they said, "All that the Lord has said we will do, and be obedient" (Ex. 24:5-7).

Then, standing before that great multitude, "Moses took the blood, sprinkled it on the people, and said, 'This is the blood of the covenant which the Lord has made with you according to all these words' " (Ex. 24:8).

Even the written covenant itself was consecrated. The writer of Hebrews says that "he took the blood of calves and goats, with water, scarlet wool, and hyssop, and sprinkled both the book itself and all the people" (Heb. 9:19).

When we honor our covenant with God, God will honor us. The remarkable story of Israel's wandering in the desert gives testimony to that fact.

[He] fed you with manna...Your garments did not wear out on you, nor did your foot swell these forty years (Deut. 8:3-4).

Why did God protect and provide for the children of Israel? Because they were a covenant people.

In the next chapter I want to show you how the blood of Jesus protects us from satan today.

FIVE

THE PROMISE
OF PROTECTION

IN 1975, ABOUT a year after I began preaching, I was invited to travel to the east coast of Florida to minister. One of the services was held at Indian Harbor Beach, Florida, in the home of my friend John Arnott, who is now the pastor of Vineyard Christian Fellowship in Toronto.

At the conclusion of my remarks I invited those who needed prayer to come forward. One woman brought her teenage daughter and asked me to pray for the girl. Just as I started to pray, I heard the clear voice of the Lord instruct me to do something I did not understand. He said, "Get the ring off her finger."

I was perplexed and thought, What does the ring have to do with my praying for her?

The Lord spoke again, even stronger. It was a command. "Get the ring off her finger."

I began questioning the voice. I wondered, Is this really God?

When I looked into the face of the young woman, I could see a soul that was in deep bondage. When God spoke those words again, I reached out and took her by the hand and asked, "What is this ring you are wearing?"

Then I lifted her hand to get a closer look at the silver band around her finger. It had a little snake engraved on it — with the head showing and the body coiled around the band. When I glanced back at her, she had a puzzled expression on her face, as if to say, What difference does it make? Go ahead and pray for me.

I was more bewildered than she was. All I knew was that the Lord had said, "Get the ring off."

I can still vividly recall this unusual encounter. I took my thumb and two fingers and tried to slide the ring from her finger. It was a loose-fitting ring, but somehow it would not budge. As I continued to pull, she began to scream. It was a loud, terrifying shriek. All the muscles in her body tightened.

Then an ugly, guttural voice spoke through her, chilling me to the marrow. "Leave her alone!" the voice shouted. "She's mine!"

The moment I heard those words I knew God had

given me the right instructions.

Holy anger surged within me because I knew I was in a battle against the power of satan. I continued to pull on the ring. Two of the men in the room could see what was happening and held my shoulders as I waged this frightening, but necessary, battle for fifteen to twenty minutes.

Over her screams I finally cried, "I apply the blood of Jesus Christ!"

And the moment I said those words the ring came off her finger. Her rigid body relaxed, and her screeching turned into a sigh of relief. She was completely delivered and asked Christ to come into her heart. I believe the power of the blood of Jesus Christ cancels out any covenant made with the power of hell.

You may say, Benny, do you believe the ring had anything to do with her condition? Yes. Because that ring symbolized her rebellion against God, I believe it was a symbol of a commitment to the forces of evil. The story of one of Israel's worst defeats helped me to understand the danger of objects that we keep in disobedience to God's commands.

Get Rid of It!

In the famous victory of the Israelites over Jericho, God instructed Joshua to tell his army not to take any of the plunder. He told them to avoid taking Jericho's riches, "lest you become accursed when you take of the accursed things, and make the camp of Israel a curse, and trouble it" (Josh. 6:18).

During their next battle at the city of Ai, Joshua's

men were about to be routed. Joshua tore his clothes and asked the Lord why.

The Lord told him:

> Israel has sinned, and they have also transgressed My covenant which I commanded them. For they have even taken some of the accursed things, and have both stolen and deceived; and they have also put it among their own stuff (Josh. 7:11).

The offending soldier was Achan, of the tribe of Judah.

> And Achan answered Joshua and said, "Indeed I have sinned against the Lord God of Israel, and this is what I have done: When I saw among the spoils a beautiful Babylonian garment, two hundred shekels of silver, and a wedge of gold weighing fifty shekels, I coveted them and took them" (Josh. 7:20-21).

It was only when Achan, his family and the stolen items were destroyed that the curse on Israel was lifted and the covenant restored. Joshua and his men were able to capture the city of Ai (Josh. 7:25; 8:1-28).

God's message is clear. Be careful of what you allow into your home, for some things bring bondage. To Achan it was a Babylonian garment. To the girl in Florida it was a satanic ring.

I believe God's protection is lifted when you possess something that goes against His commands. The passage in Joshua 7:10-12 is very clear that you should not have an accursed thing in your home. God said to the children of Israel:

> Neither will I be with you anymore, unless you destroy the accursed from among you (Josh. 7:12).

If you travel to places such as the Philippines or Africa as I have, you see firsthand the power that satanic objects have.

Of course, in America I believe people also open themselves to demonic power every time they read their horoscopes, call a psychic hot line, have their palms read, watch demonic programs and movies or play certain board games.

These things open the door to demonic activity. My strong advice to you is to read your Bible and listen to the voice of the Holy Spirit to avoid these things.

If you possess something God does not condone, get rid of it.

Protection From Plagues

The Egyptian plagues show how God will protect those who have made a blood covenant with Him.

When the children of Israel were still slaves in Egypt, they cried to the Lord for deliverance. The Lord raised up Moses, who went before Pharaoh and told him, "The Lord God of the Hebrews has sent me to you, saying, 'Let My people go' " (Ex. 7:16).

But Pharaoh refused.

That same day God turned the Nile River into blood, but Pharaoh would not listen (Ex. 7:20).

Then the Lord sent plagues of frogs, gnats, flies, livestock disease, boils, hail, locusts and darkness over the land.

Finally God told Moses to warn Pharaoh about one more plague.

> I will go out into the midst of Egypt; and all the firstborn in the land of Egypt shall die, from the firstborn of Pharaoh who sits on his throne, even to the firstborn of the female servant who is behind the handmill (Ex. 11:4-5).

Again, Pharaoh refused to let the people go.

God told Moses that the time had come for the deliverance of the children of Israel. It was such a momentous event that even their calendar should be changed. The Lord said, "This month shall be your beginning of months; it shall be the first month of the year to you" (Ex. 12:2).

God said, "This is your beginning," even though they were leaving a land that had been almost destroyed.

The Lord told Moses how the children of Israel would be spared from the death of the firstborn.

Each family was to follow these seven instructions:

1. Choose a one-year-old male lamb or goat without blemish (Ex. 12:3-5).

2. Join together with small families that cannot use a whole lamb (Ex. 12:4).

3. Keep the lamb for four days before slaughter (Ex. 12:6).

4. Have the head of the household slay the lamb on the evening of the fourteenth day of the month (Ex. 12:6).

5. Sprinkle the blood of the lamb on the sides and the tops of the door frames of the house (Ex. 12:7).

6. Roast the lamb that evening, and eat it with bitter herbs and unleavened bread (Ex. 12:8).

7. Eat the meal in haste, with your cloaks tucked into your belts, sandals on your feet and staves in your hands (Ex. 12:11).

God told them to prepare because He would pass over the land.

For I will pass through the land of Egypt on that night, and will strike all the firstborn in the land of Egypt, both man and beast; and against all the gods of Egypt I will execute judgment: I am the Lord (Ex. 12:12).

Then the Lord gave this promise:

Now the *blood* shall be a sign for you on the houses where you are. And when I see the *blood*, I will pass over you; and the plague shall not be on you to destroy you when I strike the land of Egypt (Ex. 12:13, italics added).

At midnight on the night of the Passover, the first-born in every Egyptian household died. The wailing was heard across the land even before the sun rose (Ex. 12:29-30). But in the houses of the Israelites there was not one dead.

That first Passover was a shadow of what was to happen one day on a hill called Calvary. For at Calvary "Christ, our Passover, was sacrificed for us" (1 Cor. 5:7). There we were redeemed "with the precious blood of Christ, as of a lamb without blemish and without spot" (1 Pet. 1:19).

Help for Your Household

Why did the Lord tell the Israelites to find a lamb for each household (Ex. 12:3)? I believe it is because the blessings of God's covenant can lead to salvation for an entire family.

Do you remember what God told Noah? He said, "Come thou and all thy house into the ark; for thee have I seen righteous before me in this generation" (Gen. 7:1, KJV). Noah was the only pure and virtuous man the Lord could find. Yet God told him that his entire household would find protection because of his actions.

Also, in Genesis 19:29 we find that God delivered Lot out of Sodom because of His covenant with Abraham. The passage says, "God remembered Abraham, and sent Lot out of the midst of the overthrow" (Gen. 19:29).

Centuries later, the Philippian jailer asked Paul and Silas, "Sirs, what must I do to be saved?" (Acts 16:30).

They told him, "Believe on the Lord Jesus Christ, and you will be saved, you and your household" (Acts 16:31).

I believe the Lord places special grace and protection on an entire house because of one person who comes into His kingdom (see 1 Cor. 7:14).

Let me tell you how it happened in my own life.

THE BLOOD
APPLIED

I DID NOT realize it at the time, but from the days of my childhood in Israel our family was involved in activities that were more pleasing to satan than to God. I can still remember what we called "walking through fire." A small flame was lit in a container, and incense was placed on it. All the children in our home would then step across it. We were taught that such practices would keep evil away.

Even after I became a Christian, my parents continued the practice in our home. I was the only one to oppose it.

Regularly, a fortune-teller visited our house to read my mother's palm. In Toronto a woman named Victoria would often read her coffee cup.

Most Israelis drink strong coffee in little cups. After the coffee is gone, little grounds remain. By tipping the cup over, the grounds form a pattern. The woman, supposedly an expert in such matters, came by to read the pattern and predict what was going to happen.

When I tried to warn my family that these activities were dangerous, they only laughed at me.

I remember one night in particular, more than two years after I gave my life to Christ, when I came home from church. An unusual, oppressive feeling was in the house. When I got into bed I heard noises downstairs — the refrigerator door being slammed shut, dishes breaking and the sound of horrible laughter.

Immediately I said, "Lord, cover me with Your blood. Please protect me."

Then I heard footsteps running through the back door and out of the house.

I went downstairs. No one was there. Some may not understand this, but demon power is very real. The Scriptures have a lot to say about how demons operate. Matthew 12:43-45 indicates that demons:

- get tired,

- have memories,

- have intelligence and

- work together.

Many other stories in the Gospels and Acts show us they are real (Luke 4:36; 8:26-37; Acts 19:13-16). But remember, through the Lord Jesus Christ and His mighty name we have power over them. Luke 10:19 says:

> Behold, I give you the authority to trample on serpents and scorpions, and over all the power of the enemy, and nothing shall by any means hurt you.

Furthermore, John wrote:

> He who is in you is greater than he who is in the world (1 John 4:4).

After that incident, I began to pray with great fervor that every member of my family would find Christ.

Then one day the Lord said to me, "Use your authority as a believer." He was telling me that as a Christian I had authority over satan.

As it says in Revelation 12:10-11:

> The accuser of our brethren, who accused them before our God day and night, has been cast down. And they overcame him by the blood of the Lamb and by the word of their testimony.

I began to command satan to take his hands off my family.

I learned later that on that same night the Lord appeared to my mother in such a powerful dream that she stopped inviting fortune-tellers to our home.

It was not long until both of my parents came to a little church to hear me preach the gospel. When I returned home after the service, they were waiting for me. My father asked, "Benny, how can we know this same Jesus you know?"

I was able to lead my parents to Christ. And, one by one, all of my brothers and sisters were born into the family of God.

As believers we need to command satan to take his hands off our family and off those we love.

You may have members of your family who are unsaved. Don't be discouraged. Because of you a special grace rests on your household that is more powerful than anything we can perceive.

A Hedge of Protection

When you ask God to cover your family with the blood of His Son, I believe the Lord then builds a hedge of protection around your home. That is what He did for Job.

The Bible states that Job was a righteous man, "blameless and upright, and one who feared God and shunned evil" (Job 1:1). God made him a prosperous man, with thousands of sheep, camels, oxen and other possessions. He was called "the greatest of all the people of the East" (Job 1:3).

But Job was concerned about the lifestyles of his children. His seven sons would take turns holding feasts in their homes, and they would invite their three sisters to eat and drink with them.

Job was so troubled about their spiritual condition that when the days of feasting were over:

Job would send and sanctify them, and he would rise early in the morning and offer burnt offerings according to the number of them all. For Job said, "It may be that my sons have sinned and cursed God in their hearts." Thus Job did regularly (Job 1:5).

One day some angels presented themselves to the Lord, and satan was among them.

And the Lord said to Satan, "From where do you come?"

So Satan answered the Lord and said, "From going to and fro on the earth, and from walking back and forth on it."

Then the Lord said to Satan, "Have you considered My servant Job, that there is none like him on the earth, a blameless and upright man, one who fears God and shuns evil?"

So Satan answered the Lord and said, "Does Job fear God for nothing? Have You not made a hedge around him, around his household, and around all that he has on every side?" (Job 1:7-10).

Job did exactly what God had instructed. He applied the blood, and he did it "regularly" (Job 1:5).

Do you realize that through prayer the blood can be applied for your family? God will honor *your* faith.

Job covered his family with the blood by sacrificing. In the New Testament the sacrifice has been made once and for all through Jesus Christ. So how do we take advantage of what He has done for us?

First, we must believe in the sacrifice He already made, the blood He already shed. When we believe, then we can speak it to God in prayer. The apostle Paul said, "We also believe and therefore speak" (2 Cor. 4:13). But there is no magic formula or phrase that activates the power of the blood. It is only by faith in Jesus.

Applying the Blood Through Prayer

Do you want to live in victory and be free from bondage? The key is to obey God's Word.

Prior to the first Passover, the Lord said: "The blood shall be to you for a token upon the houses where ye are" (Ex. 12:13, KJV). The word *token* means an "evidence," or a "sign" in the Hebrew. God protected the households that had the sign. And when He sees the sign, He will protect you.

People have asked, "Why should we ask God to cover us with the blood every day? Isn't this vain repetition? Aren't we being superstitious? Aren't we acting out of bondage?"

I don't pray every day because I must pray. I commune with the Lord because I love Him and want to talk with Him on a daily basis. I also ask the Holy Spirit to fill me anew every day. Asking the Lord to cover me with the blood continually is not because of bondage — but because of fellowship.

As Kathryn Kuhlman once said, "We don't live on yesterday's glories, nor on tomorrow's hopes, but on today's experiences."

You may ask, What do you mean by being covered

with the blood? It means we are appropriating all of the benefits of the cross of Jesus Christ: protection, access, forgiveness, security in God's grace, redemption, reconciliation, cleansing, sanctification, dwelling in God's presence and victory.

I don't become born again daily. But every morning I surrender again my body and mind to Him. Asking Him to cover me with His blood is not a ritual but the result of a relationship He has with me through the blood covenant.

The blood does not cover you automatically. God does not reach down from the sky and place the mark on your dwelling place. You have to ask for His protection. Remember that God *supplies*, but we *apply* through our believing prayer. The children of Israel took the blood "and put it on the two doorposts and on the lintel of the houses" (Ex. 12:7).

Forever!

The Word of God is indispensable to our knowledge and to our faith in God. And we need to gain the greatest knowledge of the Word that is possible. The Word and the blood work together. The Word *says*, and the blood *does*.

The evil one may fight you at every turn, but when you apply the blood, God's power comes alive.

As a minister, I have preached on countless topics, but each time I preach on the blood, three things happen.

- Satan makes every attempt to distract me from my preparation on the topic.

- The devil tries his best to disturb the meeting itself.

- There is an unusual presence of the Lord that accompanies the message, and a large number of people find Christ as Savior.

Just as some ministers have never preached a sermon on the blood, some Christians have rarely uttered the word *blood* since their conversions. The subject seems to be totally erased from their minds.

But God specifically instructed the Israelites to observe the Passover "as an ordinance for you and your sons forever" (Ex. 12:24).

Forever means *forever!*

The Lord has never changed His mind about His blood covenant with His people. It was not limited to the forty years that the children of Israel journeyed to the promised land. The command was in effect even after they reached their destination.

> It will come to pass when you come to the land which the Lord will give you, just as He promised, that you shall keep this service (Ex. 12:25).

We have even more to celebrate. God replaced the blood of sheep and goats with the perfect sacrifice, the blood of His Son. By the same token we are to celebrate His covenant forever.

You may ask, Benny, how often should we ask God to cover us with the blood?

I personally do it every time I pray.

There is not a day that I do not in prayer say, "Lord,

cover Suzanne, Jessica, Natasha, Joshua and Eleasha with Your blood." I do the same thing with each one of them separately. If I'm traveling, I call them on the phone and pray with them and continually pray that nothing will come into their hearts and minds but what is of the Lord.

One night I overheard little Tasha praying. She didn't know I was listening. I put my head to the door that was opened slightly. I was moved as I heard her saying, "Now, Lord, You shed Your blood for us, and I ask You to cover all of us." And she prayed for us one by one. There was another time when she said, "Now, satan, you hear me real good: You can't touch me. The blood is covering me."

That's why it's so wonderful when parents ask the Lord to protect their children with the blood. Their children not only copy them but actually will ask questions about it. Then the parents have the opportunity to tell their children what the Lord has done.

Jessica is now at the age to ask, "Daddy, why do you do that?"

I am able to tell her about the Passover story and how the blood of Jesus has been shed for us. If the blood of an animal could protect a family then, how much more can the blood of Christ protect us now?

"Don't Say That!"

In 1992 I preached a crusade in the city of Manila in the Philippines. One night they brought up to the platform a young man who was deeply troubled. In most crusades in the United States, he would have been taken aside for private ministry because my staff would have sensed his spiritual condition.

Suddenly, as this young man came close to me, I could see that he was demon possessed. His eyes were glazed over, and his whole figure began changing right in front of me. The closer he came, the worse he got.

I started praying, and he fell forward. This is something I don't understand yet; but I have noticed that when I pray for someone overseas who falls forward instead of backward, there is usually a demonic element involved.

This young man got up and started coming at me. Some of my assistants were trying to hold him back, but he began throwing them out of the way. I rebuked him, but he kept coming. Finally two very strong men were able to keep him in one place, but he was still fighting hard.

I said, "Lord, cover me and everyone around me with the blood of Jesus." Then I said to him, "The blood of Jesus is against you."

The second I said that, he screamed, "Don't say that!"

So I said it again, "The blood of Jesus is against you."

In a horrible voice he screamed out, "Don't say that!"

Every time I spoke of the blood of Jesus he would have a violent reaction. Thank God, he was finally set free.

Demons recognize the power of the blood of Jesus. If demons know it, then how much more should we know it?

I believe that when we ask God to cover us with the

blood of Jesus, He honors that because it represents the name of Jesus and what that name is all about.

The power is in Jesus Christ. And we have access through prayer.

Prayer Power

A young man in my church asked recently, "What's the secret? What can I do to pray with more power?"

I told him, "Jesus gave us the answer when He said, 'If you abide in Me, and My words abide in you, you will ask what you desire, and it shall be done for you' " (John 15:7).

I said to him, "Notice what the Lord said — 'If ye abide in Me.' It's our choice then to abide. The verse goes on to say, 'And My words abide in you, you will ask....' You will ask because you have decided to abide in Him, and you have chosen His Word to abide in you. That's the secret of power in prayer."

All things are possible through prayer.

One of the greatest teachers on prayer was R. A. Torrey. Torrey, who lived from 1856 to 1928, was the pastor of the famous Moody Church in Chicago for twelve years. In my early years as a Christian, I was deeply influenced by his writings and two other great preachers — D. L. Moody and Charles Finney.

Torrey, in his book *How to Obtain Fullness of Power*, says:

> Prayer can do anything God can do; for the arm of God responds to the touch of prayer. All the infinite resources of God are at the command of prayer.[1]

74

He also says:

> There is only one limit to what prayer can do; that is what God can do. But all things are possible to God; therefore prayer is omnipotent.[2]

E. M. Bounds, a turn-of-the-century preacher who is well known for his books on prayer, said:

> Only God can move mountains, but faith and prayer move God.[3]

I believe prayer is faith passing into action. When we pray, all that God is and has becomes ours. All you need to do is ask. As the Bible says, "Ye have not, because ye ask not," (James 4:2, KJV). I've heard it said, "The strongest one in Christ's kingdom is he who is the best knocker." So start knocking and you will find (Luke 11:9-10).

God hears and answers prayers because the blood of Jesus has cleansed us of our sins and provided access to the throne of God. The Levitical instructions for cleansing leprosy, which we will look at in the next chapter, provide a wealth of insight into the power of Christ's blood.

CLEANSING
THE LEPER

WHEN GOD GAVE the ordinances in the Old Testament, He spoke to Moses regarding "the law of the leper for the day of his cleansing" (Lev. 14:2).

David Alsobrook, in his book *The Precious Blood,*[1] has some wonderful teaching about this process. His understanding of its symbolic meaning, which I'll present in the next few pages, has really inspired me to think about how these Scripture passages have special meaning for us today.

In Scripture, leprosy refers to a variety of skin diseases. It is also a symbol of sin. So the cleansing of the leper foreshadowed God's future plan to cleanse all of mankind from sin.

First, the leper to be cleansed was "brought to the priest" (Lev. 14:2).

The priest was instructed to go outside the city and "take for him who is to be cleansed two living and clean birds, cedar wood, scarlet, and hyssop" (Lev. 14:4).

Each of these elements reminds me of the work of Christ for the remission of sin. The priests going outside the camp point to Jesus being crucified outside the walls of Jerusalem. The two birds remind me of the Lord's death and resurrection. Cedar wood points to the cross and scarlet to His suffering.

Finally, hyssop symbolizes faith. David said:

> Purge me with hyssop, and I shall be clean;
> Wash me, and I shall be whiter than snow
> (Ps. 51:7).

The hyssop that was used in purification ceremonies is generally considered to be a fragrant plant from the marjoram family.[2] It symbolizes faith to me because it was used in the application of the blood (Ex. 12:22).

What happened next was amazing in light of what Christ would do at Calvary.

> Then the priest shall order that one of the birds be killed over fresh water in a clay pot.

> He is then to take the live bird and dip it, together with the cedar wood, the scarlet yarn and the hyssop, into the blood of the bird that was killed over the fresh water (Lev. 14:5-6, NIV).

When the first bird was killed, the blood was caught in an earthen vessel with water in it (see Lev. 14:5-6, NIV). This speaks of Christ's shedding His blood in an earthen vessel — His human body.

Then the priest took the living bird along with the cedar wood (Christ's cross), the scarlet (His suffering) and the hyssop (faith), and dipped them in the shed blood of the bird that was slain.

The slain bird's blood was mixed with the water in the earthen vessel, symbolizing cleansing by the Word (Eph. 5:26).

Here was the final instruction:

> Seven times he shall sprinkle the one to be cleansed of the infectious disease and pronounce him clean. Then he is to release the live bird in the open fields (Lev. 14:7, NIV).

This speaks of our sins being cleansed by the blood. Then we see the resurrection in the living bird that was released.

This cleansing ceremony is just one example of the way the old covenant foreshadows the new covenant. Paul told the Colossians that no one should judge them according to the old covenant traditions about eating, drinking and festivals (Col. 2:16), because the law was a "shadow of things to come, but the substance is of Christ" (Col. 2:17). Hebrews also says that the law had a "shadow of good things to come" but not "the very image" (Heb. 10:1).

The leper was then allowed to come into the camp (Lev. 14:8). In the same way when you have been purified by Christ's blood you are ready to enter God's kingdom.

I believe the priests sprinkled the leper with blood seven times for a prophetic reason, for we are told that the blood of Christ was shed seven different times during the hours surrounding His crucifixion.

1. His sweat. "And being in agony, He prayed more earnestly. Then His sweat became like great drops of blood falling down to the ground" (Luke 22:44).

2. His face. "I gave...My cheeks to those who plucked out the beard" (Is. 50:6).

3. His head. "When they had twisted a crown of thorns, they put it on His head, and a reed in His right hand. And they bowed the knee before Him and mocked Him, saying, 'Hail, King of the Jews!' Then they spat on Him, and took the reed and struck Him on the head" (Matt. 27:29-30).

4. His back. "Then he [Pilate] released Barabbas to them; and when he had scourged Jesus, he delivered Him to be crucified" (Matt. 27:26).

5. His hands. "For dogs have surrounded
   Me;
   The congregation of the wicked has en-
   closed Me.
   They pierced My hands" (Ps. 22:16).

6. His feet. "They pierced...My feet" (Ps.
   22:16).

7. His side. "But one of the soldiers pierced
   His side with a spear, and immediately
   blood and water came out" (John 19:34).

The Cleansing Continues

What happened after the leper was sprinkled seven
times with blood? He now can enter the camp, even as
once we are cleansed by His blood we become sons
and daughters of the living God and members of His
family.

Because of the blood of Jesus, the floodgates of
God's anointing can be released through His Holy
Spirit in our lives. That's what I learned when the
Holy Spirit visited my life.

EIGHT

TRANSFORMED BY
THE POWER

AS I WROTE in my book *Good Morning, Holy Spirit*, it was three days before Christmas 1973 when the Holy Spirit entered my bedroom in Toronto, Canada. I was only twenty-one years old and had just returned from a Kathryn Kuhlman meeting in Pittsburgh.

That night I prayed, "Holy Spirit, Kathryn Kuhlman says You are her friend." I continued slowly, "I don't think I know You." Then, with my hands raised, I asked, "Can I meet You? Can I really meet You?"

Then it happened. The Holy Spirit came into my room with such an undeniable presence that I knew God's promise of Pentecost was true. From that moment the Holy Spirit was no longer a detached, distant "third person" of the Trinity. He was real. He had a personality. He became my closest friend, comforter and guide.

Later God began to reveal to me through His Word that it was the shed blood of Christ that made it possible for the Holy Spirit to descend.

On the Day of Pentecost Peter spoke of the Lord's death and resurrection. He continued:

> Therefore being exalted to the right hand of God, and having received from the Father the promise of the Holy Spirit, He poured out this which you now see and hear (Acts 2:33).

Remember that the Lord purchased man's redemption by His atoning death and resurrection, then ascended to His Father and there presented the blood which was the evidence of redemption.

> But Christ came as High Priest of the good things to come, with the greater and more perfect tabernacle not made with hands, that is, not of this creation. Not with the blood of goats and calves, but with His own blood He entered the Most Holy Place once for all, having obtained eternal redemption (Heb. 9:11-12).

When the Father accepted the blood, I believe Christ Jesus received from the Father the gift of the Holy Spirit to pour out upon those who believed in Him.[1] And now the Holy Spirit is on earth to enable us to live the Christian life, for God speaking through Ezekiel said:

> I will give you a new heart and put a new spirit within you; I will take the heart of stone out of your flesh and give you a heart of flesh. I will put My Spirit within you and cause you to walk in My statutes, and you will keep My judgments and do them (Ezek. 36:26-27).

The Holy Spirit not only enables us to live the Christian life but will also make God's presence very real to us.

> "And I will not hide My face from them anymore; for I shall have poured out My Spirit on the house of Israel," says the Lord God (Ezek. 39:29).

I should not have been surprised when my life was completely transformed by the power of the Holy Spirit. That is exactly what happens when you meet the Spirit of God. The prophet Samuel described it to Saul this way:

> Then the Spirit of the Lord will come upon you, and you will prophesy with them and be turned into another man (1 Sam. 10:6).

A Mighty Wind

Is it really possible that the Holy Spirit can change us totally? Absolutely. If the Lord could turn mud into man by His breath, think what He can do by breathing on us again! That is what happened at Pentecost.

> And suddenly there came a sound from heaven, as of a rushing mighty wind, and it filled the whole house where they were sitting (Acts 2:2).

Those who gathered in the upper room felt the breath of almighty God. And they were transformed.

When the Holy Spirit empowers your life, you can expect three things to happen:

- The Lord will become very close to you.

- Because of that relationship, your ultimate desire will be to walk in the ways of God.

- You will be miraculously transformed into a new person.

I am convinced that the Holy Spirit, alive and present on the earth today, is the sign of the covenant God has made with us through the blood of His Son Jesus.

> In Him you also trusted, after you heard the word of truth, the gospel of your salvation; in whom also, having believed, you were sealed with the Holy Spirit of promise (Eph. 1:13).

I have met many people who pray, "Lord, send the Holy Spirit into my life! Fill me with Your power!" The Holy Spirit will come when we honor the death of Jesus Christ and His blood.

For example, in the old covenant when blood was offered, God sent fire, and His glory descended. Do you remember what occurred at the dedication of Solomon's great temple?

> When Solomon had finished praying, fire came down from heaven and consumed the burnt offering and the sacrifices; and the glory of the Lord filled the temple (2 Chron. 7:1).

What was the sign of the Holy Spirit? In the Old Testament it was often fire (Lev. 9:23-24; 1 Kin. 18:38; 2 Chron. 7:1) representing God's all-consuming holiness.

John the Baptist also prophesied:

> I indeed baptize you with water; but One mightier than I is coming, whose sandal strap I am not worthy to loose. He will baptize you with the Holy Spirit and fire (Luke 3:16).

After Jesus shed His blood at Calvary, the Holy Spirit came as fire again. The disciples were gathered together in Jerusalem, as Jesus had commanded:

> Then there appeared to them divided tongues, as of fire, and one sat upon each of

them. And they were all filled with the Holy Spirit (Acts 2:3-4).

God will fill your life with the fire and glory of His Holy Spirit when you come to Him through the blood.

Andrew Murray, a prolific Christian author who lived from 1828 to 1917, wrote about the relationship between Jesus' blood and the Holy Spirit in his book *The Power of the Blood.*

> Where the blood is honored in faith or preaching, there the Spirit works; and where He works He always leads souls to the blood.[2]

Touched by the Anointing

The Word of God declares that it is the anointing of the Holy Spirit that enables us to serve God. God told Moses:

> You shall anoint them...that they may minister to Me as priests (Ex. 40:15).

In my own ministry I am always aware of the fact that what God is doing He is doing because of His anointing. Without it I would be spiritually bankrupt.

My daily prayer is, "Lord, don't ever lift Your anointing from me." I know the danger that exists if that anointing should ever lift. I recently read a similar statement made by Dr. Billy Graham in 1950.

I have asked God that if there were ever a

day when I should stand in the pulpit without knowing the fullness and anointing of the Spirit of God and should not preach with compassion and fire, I want God to take me home to heaven. I don't want to live. I don't ever want to stand in the pulpit and preach without the power of the Holy Spirit. It's a dangerous thing.[3]

The life of Saul contains a great lesson. Saul had been selected by God, and his life had been transformed. But the day came when he chose to break the sacrificial laws God had given the Israelites. Samuel told Saul:

You have done foolishly. You have not kept the commandment of the Lord your God, which He commanded you. For now the Lord would have established your kingdom over Israel forever (1 Sam. 13:13).

Not only did the anointing leave King Saul, but something happened that was far worse.

But the spirit of the Lord departed from Saul, and an evil spirit from the Lord troubled him (1 Sam. 16:14, KJV).

The story of Samson is another example. When the Holy Spirit left his life, he became a prisoner and a slave to the Philistines and lost his sight. The Bible states that while he slept he lost the anointing (Judg. 16:18-20).

Sleeping is symbolic of prayerlessness. Saints, let's not neglect prayer nor reject His precious Word, lest we should lose His wonderful anointing on our lives. There is nothing more I desire in this life than to have His anointing, and I know that is your greatest desire also.

Remember that as you walk in obedience to God, you don't have to fear losing the anointing. You can look forward to God's blessings instead. That's what we'll see in the next step of the cleansing of the leper.

NINE

Anointed From Head To Toe

EVERY DAY I thank God for the blood of Christ. Because the blood was shed for our sins the Holy Spirit came, and today we can know God's anointing on our lives and work.

When we are empowered by the oil of the Holy Spirit, we are freed from the chains of bondage. The prophet Isaiah wrote:

It shall come to pass in that day

That his burden will be taken away from
  your shoulder,
And his yoke from your neck,
And the yoke will be destroyed because of
  the anointing oil (Is. 10:27).

Every time I am touched by the power of God I feel like the psalmist who declared, "Let God arise, let His enemies be scattered" (Ps. 68:1).

Earlier in the book we discovered how the blood brought cleansing to the leper who symbolized sinful man. But that was only the beginning. Look what happened to the leper next. The blood made it possible for him to be anointed.

When a man was allowed back in the camp (Lev. 14:8), he was directed to "take two male lambs without blemish, one ewe lamb of the first year without blemish, three-tenths of an ephah of fine flour mixed with oil as a grain offering, and one log [about two-thirds of a pint] of oil" (Lev. 14:10).

The priest was to "take one male lamb and offer it as a trespass offering" (Lev. 14:12) — as a restitution for a specific sin. "Then he shall kill the lamb in the place where he kills the sin offering and the burnt offering, in a holy place" (Lev. 14:13).

Did you notice that the man offered more sacrifices even after he was considered cleansed and allowed back into the camp?

In the same way, the Lord Jesus shed His blood once for the remission of our sins, but we continue to ask for the cleansing and protection that His blood provides. The Lord Jesus even taught His disciples to say in prayer:

And forgive us our debts,
As we forgive our debtors.
And do not lead us into temptation,
But deliver us from the evil one (Matt. 6:12-
13).

The priest applied blood to the cleansed leper three times. Again, David Alsobrook's book *The Precious Blood* gave me insight into the meaning this process has for us today.[1] I believe God had a specific purpose for each application of blood.

First, "the priest shall take some of the blood of the trespass offering, and the priest shall put it on the tip of the right ear" of the leper (Lev. 14:14).

When the blood is applied to our hearing we are shielded from the voice of our enemies. The psalmist cried out to the Lord:

Attend to me, and hear me;
I am restless in my complaint, and moan
noisily,
Because of the voice of the enemy,
Because of the oppression of the wicked;
For they bring down trouble upon me,
And in wrath they hate me (Ps. 55:2-3).

As believers we have power over verbal attacks of the enemy. The Bible says:

No weapon formed against you shall pros-
per,
And every tongue which rises against you
in judgment

91

You shall condemn.
This is the heritage of the servants of the
    Lord (Is. 54:17).

Whose tongues arise against us? The lying tongues of the Lord's enemies. But we can condemn those voices through the blood of Christ and the authority of His Word.

When someone tells me that the devil has been speaking to them, I remind them of the wonderful words of Jesus: "My sheep hear My voice, and I know them, and they follow Me" (John 10:27).

It's not the voice of satan that we should be listening for, but the voice of the Savior. That is why we need the blood applied to our hearing.

Second, the priest then reached out to the leper and placed the blood "on the thumb of his right hand" (Lev. 14:14).

Our hands represent the work that we do. It is wonderful to know that the Lord gives guidance and protection to our work. David said:

And let the beauty of the Lord our God be
    upon us,
And establish the work of our hands for us;
Yes, establish the work of our hands (Ps.
    90:17).

And God told Isaiah,

I will direct their work in truth,
And will make with them an everlasting
    covenant (Is. 61:8).

Finally, the priest applied blood to the leper "on the big toe of his right foot" (Lev. 14:14).

Our feet are symbolic of our walk with the Lord. "If we walk in the light as He is in the light, we have fellowship with one another, and the blood of Jesus Christ His Son cleanses us from all sin" (1 John 1:7).

Sprinkled and Poured

After the priest applied blood to the leper's ear, hand and foot, God said, "Now it is time for the anointing."

Here is what happened. The priest was instructed to take "some of the log of oil, and pour it into the palm of his own left hand. Then the priest shall dip his right finger in the oil that is in his left hand, and shall sprinkle some of the oil with his finger seven times before the Lord" (Lev. 14:15-16).

The anointing oil throughout Scripture represents the work of the Holy Spirit in consecrating and empowering for service.

It is essential to understand that God anoints what the blood has covered. The anointing of the Holy Spirit *follows* the blood. The anointing oil was sprinkled seven times — God's number of completion — to represent the reception of a total anointing.

What took place next may sound repetitious, but God was doing something totally new. The priest took the oil and anointed the leper's right ear, right thumb and right big toe once again.

The blood was already there, but the anointing oil was placed on *top* of it. For where you find the blood of the cross, you will find the anointing of the Holy Spirit.

I believe the anointing expands the benefits of the blood.

- When the blood is applied to our hearing, we will not hear the enemy's voice; then God brings the anointing so we can hear *His* voice.

- When the blood is applied to our hands, the devil cannot touch our work for God; then the anointing multiplies our efforts.

- When the blood is applied to our walk, then God anoints our steps so that we can walk with Him.

Our walk also needs to be washed with His Word. Jesus said:

> He who is bathed needs only to wash his feet (John 13:10).

We have been redeemed and washed by the blood, but our walk needs to be cleansed by His Word every day (Eph. 5:26). Why? Because our lives constantly touch the dirt of the world.

In the old covenant, when God told Moses to build the tabernacle, He gave him precise details regarding every aspect, including the clothing required for the priests. But they were given no instructions regarding shoes (see Ex. 39). To remind them that they were still touching the dust of the earth, they were to walk with bare feet.[2]

As Christians we are touching the world every day. That's why we need to come back to the Lord daily and say, "Cleanse me anew and wash me again."

Head to Toe

What did God command the priest to do with the remaining oil?

> The rest of the oil that is in the priest's hand he shall put on the head of him who is to be cleansed. So the priest shall make atonement for him before the Lord (Lev. 14:18).

God wants to cover us totally from head to toe with the oil of His Spirit — our thoughts, our sight, our words and our entire lives. Not only do we have the atonement of the blood, but we have the anointing of the Holy Spirit.

Many people, however, don't think they are good enough for God's anointing because of their past. Friend, let me tell you what the shed blood of Jesus does to your past.

YOUR
BURIED PAST

MILLIONS OF PEOPLE live in a never-ending cycle of hopelessness and despair because they cannot forget about yesterday. They are tormented by memories that can lead to depression, mental anguish and even suicide.

Satan understands our weaknesses. That is why he uses our past mistakes to torture and trap us. The devil's greatest weapon against us is our past.

But thank the Lord that the blood of the cross will

remove those dead works from your conscience.

> For if the blood of bulls and of goats, and the ashes of an heifer sprinkling the unclean, sanctifieth to the purifying of the flesh: how much more shall the blood of Christ, who through the eternal Spirit offered Himself without spot to God, purge your conscience from dead works to serve the living God? (Heb. 9:13-14, KJV).

Do you realize how liberating it is to be freed from your past? Can you comprehend fully what it means to live without guilt or condemnation?

Some of you may think your past is especially fouled compared to those around you. But R. A. Torrey says:

> If we could see our past as God sees it before it is washed, the record of the best of us would be black, black, black. But if we are walking in the light, submitting to the truth of God, believing in the light, in Christ, our record today is [as] white as Christ's garments were when the disciples saw Him on the Mount of Transfiguration (Matt. 17:2, Mark 9:3, Luke 9:29).[1]

Let these words sink into your heart: *The moment the shed blood of Christ has been applied to your heart, your past is buried. It is gone forever and no longer remembered in glory.* To dwell on it is an insult to God.

Appearing in Court

Imagine yourself in a courtroom. God is the judge, and you are standing before Him. In the presence of His holiness, you are overwhelmed by a relentless consciousness of your sin.

God's voice thunders out, "I know you are guilty."

You tremble, awaiting the sentence of death.

Then God continues, "You are guilty, but I declare you righteous. Your punishment is waived."

That is called justification. God gives you a new legal standing. Your slate is clean.

God declares you righteous because of what Jesus has done.

> God had passed over the sins that were previously committed, to demonstrate at the present time His righteousness, that He might be just and the justifier of the one who has faith in Jesus (Rom. 3:25-26).

The shed blood of Jesus saves us from the wrath of a Holy God poured out against sin.

> Much more then, having now been justified by His blood, we shall be saved from wrath through Him (Rom. 5:9).

R. A. Torrey makes a wonderful comparison between forgiveness and justification.

> In forgiveness we are stripped of the vile and stinking rags of our sins; in justification we

are clothed upon with the glory and beauty of Christ.[2]

I wish that every Christian understood this truth.

Twenty-Eight Years

I will never forget a letter I received from a woman who was extremely distraught. She did not give many details but wrote, "I feel so horrible about the things I have done that I want to take my life."

I noticed that there was a telephone number on the letter and said to my secretary, "I'd like to talk with this person. See if you can reach her by phone."

The secretary reached her by phone, and the woman and I talked for a few minutes. "Why are you so troubled that you would want to end your life?" I asked.

"I am ashamed to say it," she admitted, "but I have slept with five men."

"Are you born again?"

"Yes," she said.

My immediate response was, "Have you repented? Have you asked the Lord to forgive you?"

"Yes, I have," she said.

"Do you believe God has forgiven you?"

Hesitating, she replied quietly, "I'm not sure."

"You need to know what the Bible says," I told her. "If we truly repent of our sins, the blood of Christ totally cleanses us. Our past is erased. He not only forgives, but He has chosen to forget our sins."

I told her what God said in the Scriptures:

I, even I, am He who blots out your trans-
gressions for My own sake;
And I will not remember your sins.
Put me in remembrance;
Let us contend together;
State your case, that you may be acquitted
(Is. 43:25-26).

The woman said, "Oh." Then she added, "But I am
so guilt-ridden that I can't pray. I have committed too
many sins."

I could hear her crying as she continued, "I am so
condemned that I can't even go to church. I can't
worship God. I would just rather die."

"Please tell me how long ago this happened," I
interrupted her.

"It was twenty-eight years ago," she sobbed.

"Do you mean to tell me that you have been living
with this thing for that long?"

"Yes. And it is dreadful!"

I decided to get her attention. "Do you realize that
you have been grieving the Holy Spirit?"

"What did you say?" she asked.

"Every time you said, 'I don't believe Jesus will
forgive me,' that's what you were doing."

"No! No!" she cried.

"That's exactly what you've done, and if you don't
quit you will never live in victory. You are living a life
of unbelief. God has given you His promise to bury all
of your sins, and yet you don't believe it."

"What should I do?"

"Repent before the Lord and ask Him to forgive you
for not believing His promise."

I will never forget praying with her on the phone. I could sense the bondage lifting and the sunshine dawning on her life. The woman was totally set free when she accepted what Jesus had done for her on the cross and the cleansing of His blood.

When we torment ourselves for past sin, it is like telling the devil, "Don't leave. I enjoy having you around." It is your guilt that keeps him there. But if you believe the Word and ask the Lord to cleanse you, forgive you and deliver you from all sin, you will be set free from all that the enemy can bring against you.

People need to stop listening to their emotions, their "ups and downs," their evil thoughts and their so-called friends who tell them how rotten they are. They need to believe the Word when it says, "In Him we have redemption through His blood, the forgiveness of sins, according to the riches of His grace" (Eph. 1:7).

The prophet Micah says God "will subdue our iniquities" and "cast all our sins into the depths of the sea" (Mic. 7:19).

One day I was in a church in Zeist, Holland, and heard Corrie ten Boom speak. "God takes all our sins," she said, "throws them in the deepest ocean and puts up a big sign that says 'No fishing.' "

Don't you go fishing for those sins. You're forgiven.

A Clear Conscience

The memory of your past cannot be erased simply because you want it to be. You cannot be freed from a sinful life by merely saying, "I'm going to forget about it."

God said He would "purge" us. The blood will purge your conscience completely — not only your transgressions, but every thought connected with them.

Nothing but the blood of Christ can cleanse your mind from thoughts of past and present sins. Since we have "a High Priest over the house of God, let us draw near with a true heart in full assurance of faith, having our hearts sprinkled from an evil conscience" (Heb. 10:21-22).

What is an evil conscience? One that remembers yesterday and whispers, "You're a sinner."

But in heaven the Lord says, "Welcome! I have delivered you from your iniquities. You are forgiven. Only saints can enter here, and the blood has made you righteous."

To many it sounds impossible that we can stand before God with the righteousness of Christ, but it is true. Because the blood of Jesus is pure, we become pure in God's sight. The Lord cleanses our minds from the past and the present. That is why I love to sing, "There is power, power, wonder-working power in the precious blood of the Lamb."[3]

By His promise you can now say, "The blood has washed my past, and I am free!"

Satan will always attempt to torment you by asking, "But what about your past?"

You can tell him, "My past? I have no past. It is gone for good. Christ wiped the slate clean, and I'm free."

I remember a time when I took one of my favorite shirts to the laundry. "I need some help," I told the manager. "I've sent this to you twice, and this stain is still here. What's the problem?"

"Leave it here," he said. "We'll try one more time."

When I returned, he said, "Mr. Hinn, we've tried the best solvents and cleaners available, but that stain won't budge. It's permanent. I don't think it will ever come out."

But that's not the answer I received when I gave my sin-spotted life to the Lord.

We don't think of the shed blood of God's Son as a stain remover, but it is. Christ's blood is so powerful that it removes every mark and blemish of sin.

When you lived a life of sin, you were a slave. Let me show you in the next chapter what Jesus does for slaves.

BOUGHT
WITH A PRICE

DURING THE YEARS when slavery was legal in the United States, a gentleman happened upon a slave-bidding in a crowded street.

The man paused to observe the activities. As he watched from the edge of the crowd, he saw one slave after another led onto a platform, their arms and legs shackled with ropes as if they were animals.

Displayed before the jeering crowd, they were auctioned off, one by one. Some onlookers would inspect the "merchandise," grabbing disrespectfully at the women, examining the muscular arms of the men.

The gentleman studied the group of slaves waiting nearby. He paused when he saw a young girl standing at the back. Her eyes were filled with fear; she looked so frightened. He hesitated for a moment and then disappeared briefly. When he returned, the auctioneer was about to start the bidding for the young girl he had noticed beforehand.

As the auctioneer opened the bidding, the gentleman shouted out a bid that was twice the amount of any other selling price offered that day. There was silence for an instance, and then the gavel fell as "Sold to the gentleman" was heard.

The gentleman stepped forward, making his way through the crowd. He waited at the bottom of the steps as the young girl was led down to her new owner. The rope which bound her was handed to the man, who accepted it without saying anything.

The young girl stared at the ground. Suddenly she looked up and spit in his face. Silently, he reached for a handkerchief and wiped the spittle from his face. He smiled gently at the young girl and said, "Follow me."

She followed him reluctantly. As they reached the edge of the crowd, he continued to a nearby area where each deal was closed legally. When a slave was set free, legal documents, called manumission papers, were necessary.

The gentleman paid the purchase price and signed the necessary documents. When the transaction was complete, he turned to the young girl and presented the documents to her. Startled, she looked at him with uncertainty. Her narrowed eyes asked, What are you doing?

The gentleman responded to her questioning look. He said, "Here, take these papers. I bought you to set you free. As long as you have these papers in your possession, no man can ever make you a slave again."

The girl looked into his face. What was happening? There was silence.

Slowly, she said, "You bought me to set me free? You bought me to set me free?" As she repeated this phrase over and over, the significance of what had just happened became more and more real to her.

"You bought me to set me free?" Was it possible that a stranger had just granted her freedom and never again could she be held in bondage and servitude to any man? As she began to grasp the significance of the documents which she now held in her hand, she fell to her knees and wept at the gentleman's feet.

Through her tears of joy and gratitude, she said, "You bought me to set me free? . . . I'll serve you forever!"

You and I were once bound in slavery to sin. But the Lord Jesus paid the price to set us free when He shed His blood at Calvary. That's what the Bible calls *redemption.*

> In Him we have redemption through His blood, the forgiveness of sins, according to the riches of His grace (Eph. 1:7).

That's what Paul was referring to when he wrote:

> For you were bought at a price; therefore glorify God in your body and in your spirit, which are God's (1 Cor. 6:20).

The blood of Jesus was not *spilled*; it was *shed*. It was no accident. The Lord chose to die in our place, shedding His precious blood on our behalf. Jesus said of Himself:

> The Son of Man did not come to be served, but to serve, and to give His life a ransom for many (Matt. 20:28).

Why did Christ redeem us? So "that the body of sin might be done away with, that we should no longer be slaves of sin" (Rom. 6:6). That is the only way we could "be dead indeed to sin, but alive to God in Christ Jesus our Lord" (Rom. 6:11).

Every day we can rejoice — not only in what we have been redeemed *from*, but *to* what we have been redeemed. We have been set free from slavery to sin and satan. And we have been redeemed to a new liberty from sin and to a new life in Christ (2 Cor. 3:17-18).

When you have been redeemed by His blood, you can say:

> I have been crucified with Christ; it is no longer I who live, but Christ lives in me; and the life which I now live in the flesh I live by faith in the Son of God, who loved me and gave Himself for me (Gal. 2:20).

Reconciled by the Blood

Who was in most need — the slave girl or the man who bought her? The slave girl, of course. In the same way, God did not need to be reconciled to man; man needed to be reconciled to God.

> For it pleased the Father that in Him all the fullness should dwell, and by Him to reconcile all things to Himself, by Him, whether things on earth or things in heaven, having made peace through the blood of His cross.
> And you, who once were alienated and enemies in your mind by wicked works, yet now He has reconciled in the body of His flesh through death, to present you holy, and blameless, and above reproach in His sight (Col. 1:19-22).

While it was God's desire to continue in love and fellowship with man, sin has compelled Him to become an opponent. Although the love of God toward man remains unchanged, sin made it impossible for Him to admit man into fellowship with Himself.

Andrew Murray brings incredible insight to this subject in his book *The Power of the Blood.*

> Sin has had a twofold effect. It has had an effect on God as well as on man. But the effect it has exercised on God is more terrible and serious! It is because of its effect on God that sin has its power over us. God, as Lord of all, could not overlook sin. It is His

unalterable law that sin must bring forth sorrow and death [Rom. 6:23].[1]

In the old covenant, God instructed His people to offer sacrifices. These slain animals symbolically bore the punishment for sin that the people deserved. But the sacrifices had to be made over and over again.

The old covenant was the shadow (Heb. 10:1). The new covenant brought the reality. Christ died "once for all," atoning for our sins and bringing us back into fellowship with God (Heb. 10:10). Righteousness demanded it; love offered it.

Now the Lord gives us a new responsibility: to share the message of reconciliation with the world.

> Now all things are of God, who has reconciled us to Himself through Jesus Christ, and has given us the ministry of reconciliation, that is, that God was in Christ reconciling the world to Himself, not imputing their trespasses to them, and has committed to us the word of reconciliation (2 Cor. 5:18-19).

In the time of Christ, gentiles were excluded from the family of God because they were not part of the old covenant. They were known as "aliens from the commonwealth of Israel and strangers from the covenants of promise, having no hope and without God in the world" (Eph. 2:12).

But through "the blood of His cross" these two groups — the Jews and the gentiles — were made one, and He "has broken down the middle wall of separation" so "that He might reconcile them both to

God in one body through the cross, thereby putting to death the enmity" (Eph. 2:13-14,16). He made the gentiles "fellow citizens with the saints and members of the household of God" (Eph. 2:19).

Removing the walls of hostility between people and between God and people is a part of Christ's great work as mediator of the new covenant. That's a topic we will discuss in depth in the next chapter.

TWELVE

OUR MEDIATOR

I WATCHED IN amazement in the fall of 1993 as the state of Israel and the Palestinian Liberation Organization (PLO) signed an agreement that laid a framework for peace between people whose hostilities ran decades and centuries deep.

Did those two powerful leaders just happen to meet one weekend? No. That historic moment came after years of negotiating through a third party — a mediator.

Because of His shed blood, the Lord Jesus has become our mediator with the Father.

> And for this reason He is the Mediator of the new covenant, by means of death, for the redemption of the transgressions under the first covenant, that those who are called may receive the promise of the eternal inheritance (Heb. 9:15).

Mankind has always needed a mediator. Job declared, "Oh, that one might plead for a man with God" (Job 16:21).

Under the old covenant, the high priest became the legal representative of the people regarding spiritual matters. But there were some issues that he could not arbitrate. Eli, when he was the high priest of Israel, said:

> If one man sins against another, God will judge him. But if a man sins against the Lord, who will intercede for him? (1 Sam. 2:25).

Today, Christ has become our high priest through shedding His blood. That is what gives Him the authority to be our legal mediator in heaven, representing us before the Father. Because of the cross "He is the Mediator of the new covenant, by means of death, for the redemption of the transgressions under the first covenant" (Heb. 9:15).

As our mediator, Christ intercedes on our behalf. The apostle Paul wrote, "It is Christ who died, and furthermore is also risen, who is even at the right hand of God, who also makes intercession for us" (Rom. 8:34). The Greek word for intercession is *entunchano*, which means "to meet with" and "to make petition."

And because He is our high priest, sin will not defeat us — no, not on a single score. He is our high priest, ever living to make intercession for us.

> Therefore He is also able to save to the uttermost those who come to God through Him, since He always lives to make intercession for them (Heb. 7:25).

There is only one reason why Christ can be our go-between in heaven: *because He is both God and man.*

> And being found in appearance as a man, He humbled Himself and became obedient to the point of death, even the death of the cross (Phil. 2:8).

> Inasmuch then as the children have partaken of flesh and blood, He Himself likewise shared in the same (Heb. 2:14).

Only Christ can say, "I know what man is like, and I can tell you what God is like. I understand them both from the inside out." When we are being tempted, Jesus can speak to the Father and say, "I went through the same thing."

He was sinless, and yet He became our sin bearer. Instead of symbolically cleansing us from defilement, the Lord cleansed us from *actual* sin. It was through the blood of the cross that the Lord Jesus removed the obstacle which had caused an estrangement between God and man and restored our fellowship with the Father.

> For we do not have a High Priest who cannot sympathize with our weaknesses, but was in all points tempted as we are, yet without sin (Heb. 4:15).

Though Christ is "holy, harmless, undefiled, separate from sinners, and has become higher than the heavens (Heb. 7:26), He is nevertheless "touched with the feeling of our infirmities" (Heb. 4:15, KJV).

Therefore, as the writer of Hebrews says, "let us come boldly" today to His "throne of grace, that we may obtain mercy" (Heb. 4:16). This wonderful Savior does not condemn you. He loves you for He has died for you.

> For there is one God and one Mediator between God and men, the Man Christ Jesus, who gave Himself a ransom for all (1 Tim. 2:5-6).

And because of this ransom, God declares that we are free from the pit of sin and death.

> If there is a messenger for him,
> A mediator, one among a thousand,
> To show man his uprightness,
> Then He is gracious to him, and says,

"Deliver him from going down to the Pit;
I have found a ransom" (Job 33:23-24).

So come to Jesus Christ our mediator today. Jesus said, "I am the way, the truth, and the life. No one comes to the Father except through Me" (John 14:6).

Pleading Our Cases

We know that Christ is our mediator, but He does even more for us. In that role He is also our advocate, pleading and upholding our cases before the Father.

My little children, these things I write to you, so that you may not sin. And if anyone sins, we have an Advocate with the Father, Jesus Christ the righteous (1 John 2:1).

Because of the unrelenting temptation of satan, many Christians find themselves out of fellowship with the Father. That is when they need someone who will speak on their behalf.

Jesus does not plead the case of sinners. It is only when the blood has been applied to our hearts that the Lord becomes our advocate. It is then we can say, "The Lord is my helper; I will not fear" (Heb. 13:6).

Boldness by the Shed Blood

Because the Lord Jesus sits at the right hand of the Father, we can enter boldly into the throne room.

> Therefore, brethren, having boldness to enter the Holiest by the blood of Jesus, by a new and living way which He consecrated for us, through the veil, that is, His flesh, and having a High Priest over the house of God, let us draw near with a true heart in full assurance of faith, having our hearts sprinkled from an evil conscience and our bodies washed with pure water (Heb. 10:19-22).

Our boldness to enter comes only because of Christ's sacrifice, nothing else. If we are still in our sin, no amount of brazen courage can open heaven's gates. The password is: "I come by the blood." The moment you speak those words, entrance is yours.

If you long to experience the power of redemption which Jesus accomplished, notice what the passage from Hebrews 10:19-20 says about the holy of holies, which is now open to us, and the freedom with which we can enter through the shed blood of Christ.

These verses say that God has prepared four things for us.

- "The Holiest" or most holy place — the place where God dwells or resides
- The blood of Jesus
- A new and living way
- A high priest

In response, we are to "draw near" with:

- A true heart

116

- Full assurance of faith

- Hearts sprinkled from an evil conscience

- Bodies washed with pure water

The shed blood of Christ has removed any need to be timid about approaching the Lord. The Word says:

Let us therefore come boldly to the throne of grace, that we may obtain mercy and find grace to help in time of need (Heb. 4:16).

The shed blood of Christ gives us the confidence not only to approach His throne, but also to reach the lost.

After Christ returned to glory, the disciples went everywhere preaching the message of the cross. They proclaimed it without fear and were undaunted when they were cross-examined by priests at the temple in Jerusalem.

Now when they saw the boldness of Peter and John, and perceived that they were un-educated and untrained men, they marveled. And they realized that they had been with Jesus (Acts 4:13).

At the newly formed church in Jerusalem, the Christians prayed for the disciples with these words:

Lord...grant to Your servants that with all boldness they may speak Your word, by stretching out Your hand to heal, and that

signs and wonders may be done through the
name of Your holy Servant Jesus (Acts 4:29-30).

Their prayer was answered. "The place where they
were assembled together was shaken; and they were
all filled with the Holy Spirit, and they spoke the word
of God with boldness" (Acts 4:31).
So go ahead and become fearless in your faith.

The wicked flee when no one pursues,
But the righteous are bold as a lion (Prov.
28:1).

Eternal Inheritance

Christ shed His blood and became the mediator of
the new covenant so "those who are called may receive the promise of the eternal inheritance" (Heb.
9:15).
What God promised isn't just for today; it is for
eternity. That's why it is an *eternal* inheritance.
The writer of Hebrews compares the new covenant
to a last will and testament.

For where there is a testament, there must
also of necessity be the death of the testator.
For a testament is in force after men are
dead, since it has no power at all while the
testator lives (Heb. 9:16-17).

In other words, the death of Jesus Christ activated
the power of the blood that guaranteed our inheritance.

Some people have the idea that when we enter the kingdom of God, the Lord is going to judge us according to how we have lived, give us a mansion of gold, and that's it. No. The Bible says our inheritance is eternal, meaning it's an ongoing possession. When one reward is presented, I believe there will be another. It will be like a Christmas that never ends.

Scripture tells us that "eye has not seen, nor ear heard, nor have entered into the heart of man the things which God has prepared for those who love Him" (1 Cor. 2:9). Peter says it is "an inheritance incorruptible and undefiled and that does not fade away, reserved in heaven for you" (1 Pet. 1:4). I am anxious to get to glory and find out what is in store for me.

The promises of God's Word — both the Old and New Testaments — are ours when we are redeemed by the blood.

> And if you are Christ's, then you are Abraham's seed, and heirs according to the promise (Gal. 3:29).

We don't deserve an inheritance because of our works of righteousness, "but according to His mercy He saved us...that having been justified by His grace we should become heirs according to the hope of eternal life" (Titus 3:4,7).

Too many people fear that they'll never see their inheritance. That must be because they don't understand God's amazing grace.

AMAZING
GRACE

ONE DAY A man was driving his new pickup truck on a dusty New Mexico highway when he spotted a hitchhiker standing on the side of the road. The hitchhiker was carrying a large heavy bag over his shoulder and looked exhausted in the heat of the day.

The driver stopped and asked, "Where are you headed?"

"Albuquerque."

"Hop in the back, and I'll take you there," he said.

A few miles down the road the driver glanced in his rear-view mirror and was surprised to see the man sitting in the bed of the truck with his bag over his shoulder. Why doesn't he just put it down? he wondered.

Finally, he stopped his little pickup, walked back to the man and inquired, "Why don't you rest and put that bag down?"

"Oh," said the hitchhiker, "I don't want to hurt your new truck."

I have met many Christians who are a carbon copy of that man. They have the wheels of salvation beneath them, but they are still carrying their own heavy load.

Again and again Jesus says, "Put it down. I'll carry it for you."

Instead they are proud of their self-effort and say, "No, Lord. I'd rather do it my own way."

How can they believe that they have been redeemed by the blood if they are trying to win heaven by their deeds?

Rules and Regulations

For some reason, people are drawn to works. I don't understand why, but it is true.

Some false religions call for a ritual of prayer five times a day. Others tell followers to purify themselves in the waters of sacred rivers or present gifts to gold-encrusted shrines. The world says, "Work! Work! Work!"

Some denominations began with an outpouring of

the Holy Spirit and the love of God. Before long, however, the leaders added works. Legalism replaced the presence of the Holy Spirit.

The people in these churches were told, "Here is what it takes to get to heaven. If you follow these rules, you will keep your salvation, but if not, you will suffer the consequences." And they were given a one-two-three list of outward acts to perform. They followed the rules and regulations they were given because, by our very nature, human beings love works. We mistakenly believe that it is by actions that God is pleased.

When I became a Christian I was surprised to find how many in the church were bound to rituals and spiritual protocol. A dear sister once sat me down and said, "Young man, do you know it's a sin to have long hair?" And she told me exactly how God wanted me to cut my shoulder-length hair.

Many people equate holiness with a pious outward appearance, but it is primarily a work of the heart. When we have been transformed from within, then we can demonstrate a consistently changed and transformed life.

It takes some people a lifetime to realize that holiness is not produced by legalism. Legalism is of the flesh, and God has no desire for it. Instead, "right living" is the result of our response to the grace of almighty God.

It's Not Your Ability

After I met the Holy Spirit in Toronto, I spent many hours (sometimes up to eight hours a day) praying and fellowshipping with the Lord and studying His Word. One day I read a book about Martin Luther and how the Lord used him to bring the message of justification by faith to the church of his day. One portion of the book focused on Galatians, where Paul talks about how to be free from the curse of the law.

After reading that portion, I heard the Lord's voice say in my spirit, "Did you save yourself? Or was it My blood that saved you?"

"You saved me," I answered.

"Did you choose Me?" He asked.

"No, Lord, You chose me."

"Did you convict yourself of sin?"

"No, You convicted me of sin."

"Did you draw yourself to the cross?"

"No, Lord, You drew me to the cross."

Then the Lord said, "Because you had nothing to do with your salvation, you also have nothing to do with keeping yourself saved."

At that moment I realized there is nothing I can do to merit God's favor. It is not by the flesh, but by Christ's blood and grace that the work is accomplished.

It seems we all have something in us that says, "I've got to do it myself." Perhaps it is to *prove* something. But again and again we realize that in our own strength we are miserable failures. It is when we finally surrender and say, "I can't do it!" that we have taken the first step to real living.

In 1975 I was ministering at a conference in Brockville, Ontario, where David du Plessis was also speaking. I met him for the first time while riding back to our hotel after a meeting. David was a very quiet man and always carried his briefcase with him wherever he went. When we got on the elevator to go to our rooms, I must have looked like a Mexican jumping bean next to him. I could hardly contain my excitement because I was all alone with this great giant of the faith, and I had a whole list of questions that I wanted to ask.

Very respectfully I said, "Mr. Pentecost (which is how he was known by many people), I want to ask you a question. I want to please God so badly. Please tell me — how I can please God?"

David didn't respond. He was very quiet. The elevator stopped, and we stepped out and started walking down the hall. Suddenly he stopped and stuck his finger in my chest, pushing me up against a wall. He looked at me with piercing eyes and said, "Don't even try. It's not your ability. It's His in you."

I will never forget it as long as I live.

Then he said, "Good night," and picked up his briefcase and walked away while I stood there watching him. Later, he would become a very dear friend to me and a great influence on my life.

You may be struggling and agonizing over living the Christian life and trying to please God. You may feel as if you're getting nowhere. As Kathryn Kuhlman used to say, "Quit trying and surrender." That's all God asks you to do.

In his letter to the church at Ephesus, Paul explains how we receive the amazing grace of God. He starts by describing where we were before we came under grace and still followed the ways of the world. We "were dead in trespasses and sins" (Eph. 2:1) and gratified the cravings of our sinful nature, "fulfilling the desires of the flesh and of the mind, and were by nature children of wrath" (Eph. 2:3).

Because of God's great mercy and love for us, "even when we were dead in trespasses, [He] made us alive together with Christ...and raised us up together, and made us sit together in the heavenly places in Christ Jesus" (Eph. 2:5-6).

Heaven will be ours, not because of what we have done, but because of "the exceeding riches of His grace in His kindness toward us in Christ Jesus" (Eph. 2:7). "For by grace you have been saved through faith, and that not of yourselves; it is the gift of God, not of works, lest anyone should boast" (Eph. 2:8-9).

The blood of Christ covers our sin, and we receive forgiveness through faith because of the grace of God. It is a message that every believer needs to understand.

We had nothing to do with earning our salvation. We have nothing to do with keeping it. Every time we say, "There is something I must do," God says, "I've done it. All you need to do is accept it."

Religion says, "Do." Jesus says, "Done."

When Jesus shed His blood on the cross, He said, "It is finished" (John 19:30). He didn't say, "To be continued." He is "the First and the Last" (Rev. 1:17) and "the author and finisher of our faith" (Heb. 12:2).

Because of the blood of the cross, you are no longer under law but under grace (Rom. 6:14). Your past was erased. You are free from guilt and have victory over satan.

The Lord has provided you with "a better covenant, which was established on better promises" (Heb. 8:6).

You are delivered from guilt and condemnation because the blood of Jesus Christ has been shed for your freedom and liberty (Rom. 6:18; Gal. 5:1). It's yours through God's grace.

When this truth gets into your soul, you'll never ask again, "Have my sins really been blotted out?"

Fear and Faith

Many Christians today have the wrong picture of God.

From their childhood they have built an image of an almighty God who is harsh and austere — with glaring eyes of steel. They see Him with a whip in His hand, ready to beat them every time they make the slightest mistake.

But God is nothing like that. Though He occasionally chastises us for our good, He is always gentle, kind and loving to His children.

I love what it says in the great hymn "Praise My Soul, the King of Heaven."

> Father-like, He tends and spares us;
> Well our feeble frame He knows,
> In His hands He gently bears us,
> Rescues us from all our foes.[1]

In that same hymn he says, "He's slow to chide and swift to bless." That's just what Psalm 103:8 says:

> The Lord is merciful and gracious,
> Slow to anger, and abounding in mercy.

Those who continually approach the Lord and say, "I'm filthy. I'm a failure," do not know what the grace of God is all about. When you are bound by law, the entire focus of your life is sin. Yes, we need to confess our sins to Christ and ask for forgiveness, but there is a great difference between coming before Him with fear and entering His presence with confidence.

Beneath our confession there needs to be a tremendous faith that what He did at Calvary was not for our judgment, but for our freedom. Stop looking at your failures and see God's mercy. He doesn't want to cast you aside but desires to hold you in His arms and say, "I love you."

For more than twelve hurdred years the children of Israel followed rituals and sacrifices to atone for their sin. But their focus turned from the Law-Giver to the law, and they fell into bondage.

God repeatedly tried to call them back. He was saying, "What matters is your hearts — not your works. I want you to love Me — then you will obey Me."

You may say, I thought the Old Testament dealt only with law, not love.

It doesn't. Moses told the Israelites:

> Therefore you shall love the Lord your God, and keep His charge, His statutes, His judgments, and His commandments always (Deut. 11:1).

God gave Israel a condition to His promise that the land would be fruitful for them. This condition was based on love — not works.

> And it shall be that if you earnestly obey
> My commandments which I command you
> today, to *love the Lord your God* and serve
> Him with all your heart and with all your
> soul, then I will give you the rain for your
> land in its season, the early rain and the
> latter rain, that you may gather in your
> grain, your new wine, and your oil. And I
> will send grass in your fields for your live-
> stock, that you may eat and be filled (Deut.
> 11:13-15).

God focused on love, not law, because it wasn't just difficult for the children of Israel to obey the law; it was impossible. For the Scriptures state:

> A man is not justified by the works of the law
> but by faith in Jesus Christ...for by the works
> of the law no flesh shall be justified (Gal.
> 2:16).

It is impossible to obey the will of God with our own strength. As my father-in-law, Roy Harthern, used to say, "Living the Christian life isn't difficult; it's impossible." But God sent the Holy Spirit to live in our hearts and enable us to obey His commands. God told His people through Ezekiel, "I will put My Spirit within you and cause you to walk in My statutes, and you will keep My judgments and do them" (Ezek. 36:27).

Even the early believers had to learn the fact that we are not justified by works but by faith in God. In Acts 15:1 the story is told of certain men which "came down from Judea and taught the brethren, 'Unless you are circumcised according to the custom of Moses, you cannot be saved.' "

Do or Die!

Some of the disciples were sent to Jerusalem to address the issue. After much discussion, Peter stood and said:

> Men and brethren, you know that a good while ago God chose among us, that by my mouth the Gentiles should hear the word of the gospel and believe. So God, who knows the heart, acknowledged them [the Gentiles], by giving them the Holy Spirit, just as He did to us, and made no distinction between us and them, purifying their hearts by faith (Acts 15:7-9).

The law required circumcision, but all the new covenant demanded was faith.

Remember, law and works have always been the opposite of grace and mercy.

- The law says, "Follow the rules." Grace says, "It is a free gift."

- The law says, "See your sin and shame." Grace says, "God accepts you as you are."

- The law brings the consciousness of sin. Grace brings the awareness of righteousness.

- The law says, "Do or die." Grace says, "Accept Jesus as Savior and live."

The Vine and the Branches

It is not our strength that produces life, but His.

Just before the crucifixion, Jesus had a meal with His disciples and gave them one of the greatest lessons found in the Gospels. He told them that they were not the vine, and they were not the fruit — they were the *branches*.

We are an *outlet* for God's power, not the power itself. Jesus said:

> I am the true vine, and My Father is the vinedresser. Every branch in Me that does not bear fruit He takes away; and every branch that bears fruit He prunes, that it may bear more fruit. You are already clean because of the word which I have spoken to you. Abide in Me, and I in you. As the branch cannot bear fruit of itself, unless it abides in the vine, neither can you, unless you abide in Me.
>
> I am the vine, you are the branches. He who abides in Me, and I in him, bears much fruit; for without Me you can do nothing (John 15:1-5).

God's purpose as the "vinedresser" is to keep the vine clean. The pruning of sin is not the result of our effort, but of His. All we are required to do is surrender.

Some Christians are struggling to bear fruit, but no branch has the power to make that happen. Jesus was saying, "You don't bear the fruit. I do. But I give you the privilege of holding it. The fruit is Mine. The vine is Mine. The branch is simply hooked onto Me. That's all."

Someone once asked, "If God is doing all the work, then what is my job?"

"Hang on!" I replied.

The vine supplies life to the branches, and the branch has the privilege of holding the fruit. In effect, our job is to become "fruit hangers."

Take a close look at what is attached to the branch. It is the fruit of the Holy Spirit — not of the flesh. We become the channel through which love, joy, peace and other spiritual fruit are given to the world (Gal. 5:22-23).

What is the result of our branch-vine relationship? When we understand it and make the Lord the source of our lives, He answers our prayers. Jesus said:

> If you abide in Me, and My words abide in you, you will ask what you desire, and it shall be done for you (John 15:7).

Never forget that Jesus said, "Without Me you can do nothing" (John 15:5). That is true before, during and after salvation.

The vine is strong and the branch is weak, but branches are what God uses to deliver His fruit to the world. In the words of the apostle Paul:

God has chosen the foolish things of the world to put to shame the wise, and God has chosen the weak things of the world to put to shame the things which are mighty; and the base things of the world and the things which are despised God has chosen, and the things which are not, to bring to nothing the things that are, that no flesh should glory in His presence (1 Cor. 1:27-29).

"Free Indeed"

Without the blood of Christ and God's grace it would be impossible for us to have victory over sin. Paul told what it's like to fight sin in the flesh. "For we know that the law is spiritual, but I am carnal, sold under sin" (Rom. 7:14). He added, "For I know that in me (that is, in my flesh) nothing good dwells; for to will is present with me, but how to perform what is good I do not find" (Rom. 7:18).

Our flesh contains nothing that is good, and our righteousness is as filthy rags (Is. 64:6). We can't make ourselves good enough to please God.

I remember praying, "Lord, there must be *something* I can do to please you."

"My greatest pleasure is when you allow Me to do the work," He said.

I once heard a story about a Russian pastor who was thrown in prison by communist officials for preaching the gospel in the former Soviet Union. They did not allow this great saint of God to see another human being, and they fed him by pushing the food under the door. Years and years passed, and one day the Lord appeared to this man in prison.

The man was so grateful to the Lord for coming to see him. He asked Him, "Is there anything I can give You to say thank You?"

"No, everything is Mine," the Lord responded. "There is nothing you can give Me."

"But, Lord, there must be something I can give You to say thank You."

"There is nothing you can give Me," the Lord repeated. "Your very body belongs to Me. Your very life is Mine."

But the man asked again, "Oh, please, there must be one thing I can give You."

Then the Lord said, "There is. Give Me your sins. That's all I want."

That's all He wants — our surrender. We turn our sins over to Him because He is the only one who can subdue them. The Bible says:

Who is a God like You,
Pardoning iniquity
And passing over the transgression of the
   remnant of His heritage?
He does not retain His anger forever,
Because He delights in mercy.
He will again have compassion on us,
And will subdue our iniquities (Mic. 7:18-
   19).

Paul's solution to his struggle with sin was to turn it over to Christ. He said: "For the law of the Spirit of life in Christ Jesus has made me free from the law of sin and death. For what the law could not do in that it was weak through the flesh, God did by sending His own Son in the likeness of sinful flesh, on account of sin: He condemned sin in the flesh, that the righteous requirement of the law might be fulfilled in us who do not walk according to the flesh but according to the Spirit" (Rom. 8:2-4).

Some people say, "I've tried to pray, and I have failed. I've tried to read the Word, and my mind wanders. I've tried to get rid of my habits, and I can't."

Again and again they say, "Lord, I'll try one more time." And they continue to fail.

After many years they finally pray the only prayer God wants to hear: "Lord, I can't do it. You will have to do the work." And they finally learn what Philippians 2:13 really means:

> It is God who works in you both to will and to do for His good pleasure.

Suddenly they are transformed and find how easy it is to live for Jesus. Jesus said, "My yoke is easy and My burden is light" (Matt. 11:30).

To the drug addict the Lord says, "Stop trying to set yourself free!" To the alcoholic He says, "You'll never quit on your own." To the smoker He says, "Let Me touch you and set you free."

Jesus said:

> Whoever commits sin is a slave of sin. And a slave does not abide in the house forever, but a son abides forever. Therefore if the Son makes you free, you shall be free indeed (John 8:34-36).

Saint, remember that you will never be able to solve your own problems. The Scriptures say it is "not by might nor by power, but by My Spirit" (Zech. 4:6).

Remember what Kathryn Kuhlman said: "Quit trying and surrender."

THE FATHER'S HAND

WHEN MY OLDEST daughter Jessica was just a toddler, I remember taking her for a walk in the woods.

As we were about to walk up a little hill, I reached down and took hold of her hand. I didn't want her to slip and fall.

Jessica's little hand was too weak to hold on to mine. She was depending on my strength to help her reach the top of the hill.

Then the Holy Spirit said to me, "Who is holding your hand?"

As I thought about it, I said, "You are, Lord."

How true it is. All of us are like my little girl Jessica. We're too weak to hold on to His hand. He holds on to our hands.

The Bible says, "For I, the Lord your God, will hold your right hand, saying to you, 'Fear not, I will help you' " (Is. 41:13).

The old covenant promised it, and so did the new. Jesus said, "And I give them eternal life, and they shall never perish; neither shall anyone snatch them out of My hand" (John 10:28).

The first time I read that Scripture passage I said, "Thank You, Lord, for reaching down and holding me."

Several years later, I was studying the passage again, and I began to praise the Lord as I noticed what the next verse said.

My Father, who has given them to Me, is greater than all; and no one is able to snatch them out of My Father's hand (John 10:29).

Not only is Jesus holding my hand. But the Father is holding it, too. When He reaches out to you, you can be sure that He will never let go. The only time Jesus will let you go is when you push Him away.

Not only does the Lord hold us, but He will lead us in the right path. You are God's possession, and He will protect you and sustain you. The psalmist tells us:

The steps of a good man are ordered by
the Lord,

And He delights in his way.
Though he fall, he shall not be utterly cast
  down;
For the Lord upholds him with His hand
  (Ps. 37:23-24).

For You have delivered my soul from death.
Have You not kept my feet from falling,
That I may walk before God
In the light of the living? (Ps. 56:13).

God's grace is not something that happens in a moment of time and then disappears. It is part of our process of growing. Peter said that we are to "grow in the grace and knowledge of our Lord and Savior Jesus Christ" (2 Pet. 3:18).

How is it possible to grow in grace? By learning His love, His patience, His mercy and His acceptance of us. In hundreds of ways the Lord says, "I won't give up on you. I love you and I forgive you."

When we fail, He reaches down again and takes us in His arms. That is how we continue to grow in grace.

Grace and Truth

The Word says that Christ was filled with grace and truth.

And the Word became flesh and dwelt among us, and we beheld His glory, the glory as of the only begotten of the Father, full of grace and truth (John 1:14).

Christ revealed that grace and truth to us.

> For the law was given through Moses, but grace and truth came through Jesus Christ (John 1:17).

When the Lord was teaching a group of people in the temple courts of Jerusalem, the Pharisees brought to Him a woman who had been caught in adultery. "Now Moses, in the law, commanded us that such should be stoned. But what do You say?" (John 8:5).

Jesus ignored their question and bent over to write something on the ground with His finger. When they continued questioning Him, He stood up and said, "He who is without sin among you, let him throw a stone at her first" (John 8:7).

As He continued to write on the ground, the critics began to walk away until only Jesus and the woman were left. He turned to her and asked, " 'Woman, where are those accusers of yours? Has no one condemned you?' She said, 'No one, Lord.' And Jesus said to her, 'Neither do I condemn you; go and sin no more' " (John 8:10-11).

He said, "Neither do I condemn you" — that's grace.

"Go and sin no more" — that's truth.

She saw His grace and decided to sin no more. When we truly see His love and grace, we will also want to follow Him and leave our sin.

The Lord never tells us to "sin no more" — or do any other thing — unless He knows we can do it. And because He gives us the power to obey His commands, He knows we can do it. This way, every command is really a promise.

Fear and Trembling

Every time I discuss the grace of God someone will ask, "Doesn't the Bible tell us that we have to work out our own salvation?"

Here is what Paul said: "Work out your own salvation with fear and trembling" (Phil. 2:12). But we need to look at the context of that statement.

> Therefore, my beloved, as you have always obeyed, not as in my presence only, but now much more in my absence, work out your own salvation with fear and trembling (Phil. 2:12).

But that is not the end of the story. It is not our work but the Lord's that makes it possible. The next verse says, "For it is God who works in you both to will and to do for His good pleasure" (Phil. 2:13).

So the Christian life is really working out or exercising the salvation that God has provided — and He gives us both desire and strength to do what pleases Him.

Here is the amazing thing: When we let God do the work in us, then He enables us to work out His salvation.

> For we are His workmanship, created in Christ Jesus for good works, which God prepared beforehand that we should walk in them (Eph. 2:10).

The Lord is not against our efforts, but they must be a product of His workmanship — His grace. In fact, one of the Lord's purposes for your salvation is to have you live a "blameless" life.

He chose us in Him before the foundation of
the world, that we should be holy and without blame before Him (Eph. 1:4).

Good works will be a by-product of those who
know God's unmerited favor. And the Lord gives us
the will to love Him, obey Him and serve Him. We
can't follow the Lord without His first touching us.
Jesus said, "No one can come to Me unless the Father
who sent Me draws him" (John 6:44).

We can't love Him without the Holy Spirit's giving
us the love with which to love Him.

Now hope does not disappoint, because the
love of God has been poured out in our
hearts by the Holy Spirit who was given to us
(Rom. 5:5).

When you experience God's love, you will love.
When you find His acceptance, you will accept others.
When you experience giving, you will give.

It all comes down to one simple thing: *God works it
in, and we work it out.*

We let Him pour in that we may pour out. First, we
cooperate; then we respond. But the Bible makes it
clear that we can't work to earn our salvation.

Now to him who works, the wages are not
counted as grace but as debt.

But to him who does not work but be-
lieves on Him who justifies the ungodly, his
faith is accounted for righteousness (Rom.
4:4-5).

141

The Lord does not owe us something because we do good works. He will never put Himself in debt to anyone. We don't say, "I did it, Lord. Here's my bill." If we work for something, it is not grace.

There is nothing in us that even desires God without His first putting the desire within us (John 6:44). God won't honor a person who says, "I'm going to pray, and I'm going to make it." God says, "That is the flesh, and I don't want it." God won't accept works or prayers that come from the flesh.

Total Dependence

One day as I was reading Psalm 119, I noticed the way David was saying, "I cannot do it, Lord. Only You can." I began to see in this psalm his total dependence on God.

> *Deal bountifully* with Your servant, that I
>   may live and keep Your word (v. 17).
> *Open my eyes*, that I may see wondrous
>   things from Your law (v. 18).
> I am a stranger in the earth; *do not hide*
>   Your commandments from me (v. 19).
> *Remove from me* reproach and contempt,
>   for I have kept Your testimonies (v. 22).
> My soul clings to the dust; *revive me* accord-
>   ing to Your word (v. 25).
> *Make me understand* the way of Your pre-
>   cepts; so shall I meditate on Your won-
>   derful works (v. 27).
> *Remove from me* the way of lying, and
>   *grant me* Your law graciously (v. 29).

I will run the course of Your commandments, for *You shall* enlarge my heart (v.
32).
Teach me, O Lord, the way of Your statutes,
and I shall keep it to the end (v. 33).
Give me understanding, and I shall keep
Your law; indeed, I shall observe it with
my whole heart (v. 34).
Make me walk in the path of Your commandments, for I delight in it (v. 35).
Incline my heart to Your testimonies, and
not to covetousness (v. 36).
Turn away my eyes from looking at worth-
less things, and *revive me* in Your way (v.
37).
Establish Your word to Your servant, who is
devoted to fearing You (v. 38).
Turn away my reproach which I dread, for
Your judgments are good (v. 39).
Behold, I long for Your precepts; *revive me
in Your righteousness* (v. 40).
Let my heart be blameless regarding Your
statutes, that I may not be ashamed (v.
80).
Hold me up, and I shall be safe, and I shall
observe Your statutes continually (v. 117).
Be surety for Your servant for good; *do not
let* the proud oppress me (v. 122).
Direct my steps by Your word, and *let no
iniquity have dominion over me* (v. 133).

Who is doing the work? David or the Lord?
We see clearly here that David is saying, "Only the

Lord can." All we have to do is surrender and let Him do it. So like David, ask Him today to come and work His grace in you and say, "Lord, 'direct my steps' so that I can walk with You" (see Ps. 119:133).

True prayer is impossible without the Holy Spirit's help. Like so many Christians, I thought I could seek the Lord on my own until one day I read Psalm 119:176, which states:

> I have gone astray like a lost sheep;
> Seek Your servant,
> For I do not forget Your commandments.

When it comes to seeking Him, remember that He seeks us first. As A. W. Tozer said, "Before a man can seek God, God must first have sought the man."[1]

From that day until now I pray daily, "Lord Jesus, touch me so that I can call on You. Give me the strength to seek You today."

David himself said in the Psalms, "Quicken us, and we will call upon thy name" (Ps. 80:18, KJV).

It is not your doing. It is His grace.

I heard an amazing definition of grace one night on a Christian television program. What I learned is the subject of my next chapter.

FIFTEEN

YOUR NEW FAMILY

ONE EVENING I was watching a Christian television program. A preacher was teaching about grace. He caught my attention when he said, "Let me tell you what grace really is.

"Let's suppose that a man has an only child who is murdered. The man has three choices. He can kill the man for murdering his son, which would be revenge. He can let the law deal with him, which would be justice. Or he can forgive him, adopt him and give him his son's place. Now that's grace."

That is exactly what God did when He saved you and me.

We were the ones who put His Son on the cross. It was for our sins and iniquities that Jesus shed His precious blood. And because of His sacrificial death, when we repent of our sins and accept Jesus as Savior and Lord, God forgives us. Not only that, but we have been adopted into God's wonderful family.

> Behold what manner of love the Father has bestowed on us, that we should be called children of God! (1 John 3:1).

How true are the words of the song:

> Amazing grace! how sweet the sound,
> That saved a wretch like me!
> I once was lost, but now am found,
> Was blind, but now I see.[1]

So great is the Father's grace that Jesus said, "You...have loved them as You have loved Me" (John 17:23).

And so great is His love that Psalm 139:17-18 says:

> How precious also are Your thoughts to
>   me, O God!
> How great is the sum of them!
> If I should count them, they would be
>   more in number than the sand.
> When I awake, I am still with You.

Not only does He love us, but He thinks about us all the time. The Bible says that God will never forget us.

Graven on His Palms

In Isaiah 49:15-16 the Lord says:

> Can a woman forget her nursing child,
> And not have compassion on the son of
>   her womb?
> Surely they may forget,
> Yet I will not forget you.
> See, I have inscribed you on the palms of
>   My hands.

This Scripture passage speaks of one of the customs of the East. When a mother had to be separated from one of her children, she would have the name tattooed on her palm. All her days were spent working with her hands, and the marks on her palm constantly reminded her of the child she loved and longed to see.[2]

The Lord thinks of you just as often and more.

Unfortunately, some do not know His love. They accept Him to escape hell. They accept Him on the basis of fear. They are looking for a fire escape. Those who receive Him on the basis of fear are always attempting to do something to prove they are really saved. But their fear results in futile legalism and useless works.

On the other hand, the person who accepts Christ on the basis of love discovers, "It is not what I have done, but what He has done for me." They see how loving He is.

When you see His love, you will not see defeat.

When you see heaven, you won't see hell. When you see mercy, you won't see judgment.

Most people have been in the courtroom too long. Every time they come before the Lord, they see themselves appearing before a judge. But the Word says:

> Most assuredly, I say to you, he who hears My word and believes in Him who sent Me has everlasting life, and shall not come into judgment, but has passed from death into life (John 5:24).

When Jesus hung on the cross, your sentence of death was waived. The Father took His judicial robe off, put down the gavel and said, "Come into the family room. Come home!" Instead of presiding over a court of justice, I see Him standing in the family room, waiting for His children to return.

When you repent and accept God's grace, He adopts you into His family. God did not receive you so that He could "unadopt" you later. He does not threaten to throw you out of the family. The Lord brings us in and *keeps* us in.

We Don't Deserve It

Long ago the Lord spoke through the prophet Jeremiah and said:

> They shall be My people, and I will be their God; then I will give them one heart and one way, that they may fear Me forever, for the good of them and their children after them.

And I will make an everlasting covenant with
them, that I will not turn away from doing
them good; but I will put My fear in their
hearts so that they will not depart from Me
(Jer. 32:38-40).

By any account, the children of Israel should have
perished. God even said, "The children of Israel and
the children of Judah have done only evil before Me
from their youth" (Jer. 32:30). But He didn't give them
what they deserved. He covered them with His everlasting grace and drew them by His love. Speaking to
Israel, God said:

Yes, I have loved you with an everlasting
    love;
Therefore with lovingkindness I have
    drawn you (Jer. 31:3).

It is mercy that keeps us out of hell by not giving us
the punishment we deserve. But grace gets us into
heaven by giving us *the reward we don't deserve.*

Through the Lord's mercies we are not con-
    sumed,
Because His compassions fail not.
They are new every morning;
Great is Your faithfulness (Lam. 3:22-23).

Paul wrote that "the law entered that the offense
might abound. But where sin abounded, grace
abounded much more" (Rom. 5:20). I thank God that
the blood of Christ and the grace of God are more

powerful than our iniquity. There may be a flood of sin, but there is a "superflood" of grace. And if you have repented and received this wonderful grace of God, you are forgiven and have discovered the truth of 1 Corinthians 1:27-29:

> But God has chosen the foolish things of the world to put to shame the wise, and God has chosen the weak things of the world to put to shame the things which are mighty; and the base things of the world and the things which are despised God has chosen, and the things which are not, to bring to nothing the things that are, that no flesh should glory in His presence.

Yet some say, "God helps those who help themselves." But those words cannot be found in the Word. When you think you're a little god who can solve every problem, God will leave you to your own devices. Only Christ can transform the heart of man.

Humanism says, "You are the master of your fate. You have the power to help yourself."

But Jesus said:

> The Spirit of the Lord is upon Me,
> Because He has anointed Me
> To preach the gospel to the poor;
> He has sent Me to heal the brokenhearted,
> To proclaim liberty to the captives
> And recovery of sight to the blind,
> To set at liberty those who are oppressed
>   (Luke 4:18).

We are the poor, the brokenhearted, the captive, the blind, the oppressed. God is not asking us to help ourselves. He just asks us for complete reliance on Him. The Bible does not teach independence. It proclaims *de*pendence on the Lord.

A Matter of Choice

A man once asked me, "If God does everything, how is choice involved?" It was a valid question.

"Before you were saved, did you seek the Lord or did He seek you?" I asked him.

"He sought me," he replied.

"Did you produce the faith to believe? Or did He give it to you?"

"He gave it to me."

"Well, if God did all of those things then, who is keeping you now? Are you keeping yourself? And who will take you into heaven? Can you do it yourself?" I asked. Finally I said, "You have nothing to do with it."

"All that is good, but where is choice?"

"All you need to say is yes to Jesus, and these things will be yours. Your choice is just to accept what He has done for you."

A big smile broke across his face. "I see it!"

Jesus told His disciples, "You did not choose Me, but I chose you and appointed you" (John 15:16).

But Scripture warns us that God's grace must never be misused.

> We then, as workers together with Him also plead with you not to receive the grace of God in vain (2 Cor. 6:1).

Salvation is ours because of what the Lord has done, not because of our perfection. What produces failure? It is when we stop trusting God and rely on ourselves. The prophet Ezekiel said:

> When I say to the righteous that he shall surely live, but he trusts in his own righteousness and commits iniquity, none of his righteous works shall be remembered; but because of the iniquity that he has committed, he shall die (Ezek. 33:13).

I believe that we are secure in our salvation, but we can risk losing what He has given us. For Peter said:

> For if, after they have escaped the pollutions of the world through the knowledge of the Lord and Savior Jesus Christ, they are again entangled in them and overcome, the latter end is worse for them than the beginning. For it would have been better for them not to have known the way of righteousness, than having known it, to turn from the holy commandment delivered to them (2 Pet. 2:20-21).

Where is the balance? God chooses us but always gives us the choice to respond.

If someone came to me with a gun pointed at my head and said, "Deny Christ or die," I would say, "Shoot." Why? Because my commitment to Christ is not temporary; it's eternal.

When I met the Lord it was not a "goose-bump," momentary experience. At that moment I became a totally new person. It was an instantaneous, new birth. It is a continuous salvation.

What should be our response to the Lord in return for His eternal benefits? The psalmist said: "I will take up the cup of salvation, and call upon the name of the Lord" (Ps. 116:13).

> Gracious is the Lord, and righteous;
> Yes, our God is merciful.
> The Lord preserves the simple;
> I was brought low, and He saved me.
> Return to your rest, O my soul,
> For the Lord has dealt bountifully with you
> (Ps. 116:5-7).

This salvation is even better than we can think. We can have complete confidence that He will finish what He has started...that He has committed to keep us (Phil. 1:6). But how can we know that in our hearts? The answer lies in understanding the seal of the Holy Spirit.

THE GREAT SEAL

WHEN WE ARE washed by His blood and cleansed by the Word, then the Lord puts the seal of the Holy Spirit on us. Paul wrote:

In Him you also trusted, after you heard the word of truth, the gospel of your salvation; in whom also, having believed, you were sealed with the Holy Spirit of promise, who is the guarantee of our inheritance until the redemption of the purchased possession, to the praise of His glory (Eph. 1:13-14).

A seal is a symbol of protection. It says, "This is mine. Put it aside, and leave it for me. No one is to touch it because I am coming back to claim it."

The Lord does not seal anything that He does not plan to redeem. And He would not build mansions unless He was waiting for us to come home (John 14:2-3).

We will remain sealed until Christ takes us home "to an inheritance incorruptible and undefiled and that does not fade away, reserved in heaven for you" (1 Pet. 1:4).

The inheritance is for those "who are kept by the power of God through faith for salvation ready to be revealed in the last time" (1 Pet. 1:5).

The seal will not be removed until His final work has been completed. Paul said that we "who have the firstfruits of the Spirit, even we ourselves groan within ourselves, eagerly waiting for the adoption, the redemption of our body" (Rom. 8:23).

The work is complete when the final trumpet sounds.

> The dead will be raised incorruptible, and we shall be changed. For this corruptible must put on incorruption, and this mortal must put on immortality. So when this corruptible has put on incorruption, and this mortal has put on immortality, then shall be brought to pass the saying that is written: "Death is swallowed up in victory" (1 Cor. 15:52-54).

Seventy Times Seven

As long as you accept what Christ's blood has done for you, no power on earth can break God's seal (2 Tim. 1:12).

> For I am persuaded that neither death nor life, nor angels nor principalities nor powers, nor things present nor things to come, nor height nor depth, nor any other created thing, shall be able to separate us from the love of God which is in Christ Jesus our Lord (Rom. 8:38-39).

You may ask, Are you telling me that God loves me in spite of myself?

Yes. Regardless of our inconsistencies, He still loves us. He adopted us even though we were responsible for the death of His Son. And He welcomes us back even when we falter and fail.

Some people worry, What if I make the same mistake again and again? Will He still pardon me?

Peter asked Jesus the same question.

> "Lord, how often shall my brother sin against me, and I forgive him? Up to seven times?" Jesus said to him, "I do not say to you, up to seven times, but up to seventy times seven" (Matt. 18:21-22).

The Lord's answer does not mean Christians can live in sin without repenting and still make heaven. Far from it. Those who abuse the forgiving nature of

God have never experienced His true salvation. What God offers is more than eternal security — He gives us eternal grace.

It is God's transforming grace that makes redemption possible and prepares us to live godly lives.

> For the grace of God that brings salvation has appeared to all men, teaching us that, denying ungodliness and worldly lusts, we should live soberly, righteously, and godly in the present age, looking for the blessed hope and glorious appearing of our great God and Savior Jesus Christ, who gave Himself for us, that He might redeem us from every lawless deed and purify for Himself His own special people, zealous for good works (Titus 2:11-14).

When you come face to face with the saving grace of God, it will bring a hunger for righteousness and godliness.

Because of the finished work of Calvary, God sent His Holy Spirit to provide strength to live holy lives. Paul said that we "do not live according to the sinful nature but according to the Spirit" (Rom. 8:4, NIV).

What God said to the prophet Zechariah is still true.

> "Not by might nor by power, but by My
> Spirit,"
> Says the Lord of hosts.
> "Who are you, O great mountain?
> Before Zerubbabel you shall become a
> plain!

157

And he shall bring forth the capstone
With shouts of 'Grace, grace to it!' " (Zech.
    4:6-7).

You may be facing temptation that seems like a
mountain that will crush you. But because of the Spirit
of the Lord and because of His grace, you can take
that mountain apart stone by stone.

The Power of Grace

With God's grace comes great power.

> With great power the apostles gave witness
> to the resurrection of the Lord Jesus. And
> great grace was upon them all (Acts 4:33).

In the book of Acts we see what the power of God
accomplished in the first Christians.

• They received power and became witnesses. "But
you shall receive power when the Holy Spirit has
come upon you; and you shall be witnesses to Me"
(Acts 1:8).

• The Holy Spirit changed their speech. They began speaking in unknown tongues (Acts 2:4) and
speaking God's word with boldness (Acts 4:31).

• Their demeanor was changed. Stephen was the
most dramatic example of this. When the Holy Spirit
came upon Stephen while he was on trial, "all who sat
in the council, looking steadfastly at him, saw his face
as the face of an angel" (Acts 6:15). I believe that
when God's anointing is on someone, the presence of
the Holy Spirit is evident to those around that person.

There is a look of divine power and joy on his or her face, a sense of authority in the person's voice. That's why Peter and John told the lame man, "Look at us" (Acts 3:4). When that lame man looked at them, they knew he would be able to see that the power of God was upon them.

One of the things I will never forget about Kathryn Kuhlman is that every time the anointing came on her, her eyes would change. They would have a sparkle in them.

I've noticed something over the years. Any time the anointing leaves a servant of God, the sparkle goes; the fire goes. I recall a man who came to visit my church recently. At one time he was one of the mightiest men of God in Canada. But when I looked at him, there was no sparkle, no fire anymore. The anointing was gone, and his face showed it.

• The Holy Spirit gave them boldness. "Now when they saw the boldness of Peter and John, and perceived that they were uneducated and untrained men, they marveled" (Acts 4:13). They had no more fear, but glorious boldness to proclaim the good news of the gospel.

• The Holy Spirit changed their relationships. Peter said that he was a witness of what Jesus had done "and so also is the Holy Spirit" (Acts 5:32). Here we see the Holy Spirit as their companion and helper.

• The Holy Spirit changed their position. Stephen started out as an usher in the church (Acts 6:5), but he ended up being a mighty evangelist (Acts 6:8-10).

• The Holy Spirit changed their vision. "But he, being full of the Holy Spirit, gazed into heaven and saw the glory of God, and Jesus standing at the right hand of God" (Acts 7:55).

The Holy Spirit's great power is available to us today because we have also received God's "great grace."

The Holy Spirit in our lives is a reminder that Christ has bled and died, risen again and ascended to the right hand of His Father. Jesus Himself asked His disciples to remember Him in another special way. My eyes were opened to a rich, new meaning in this remembrance by a group of charismatic nuns.

THE COMMUNION
IN THE COMMUNION

A COUPLE OF years ago I held a crusade where more than twelve thousand people jammed a coliseum at a fairgrounds to hear the Word of God preached.

As I ministered on the platform, my eyes were drawn to a group of Roman Catholic nuns dressed in distinctive floor-length black habits sitting down front in the massive crowd.

Because I was taught by Catholic nuns when I was

a boy, I have a special place in my heart for them. So I called them — forty-nine in all — up onto the platform. We talked, and I discovered they were Catholic charismatics who had driven six hours to attend the service.

I invited them to join me in leading the people in a rousing version of "How Great Thou Art." At the end of the song, the nuns pulled their crosses out from under their habits and lifted them toward the Lord. It was a very powerful moment, one I'll never forget.

After the service I had a little more time to talk with them. I learned they belonged to an order which was founded by their mother general, a tall woman with piercing blue eyes. (I found out later that a mother general is even higher than a mother superior.)

"Why don't you come and visit our convent?" the mother general asked me.

"I would love to come," I told her.

A few months later I did. The convent is located on rolling hills in a river valley. The sisters built all of the buildings including a retreat center and a farm where they raise their own animals.

The sisters served me and a few friends who had accompanied me a beautiful turkey dinner, complete with vegetables they had grown themselves.

After dinner they asked, "Would you mind if we served you communion?"

"Not at all. I would love it," I said.

(Apparently, they felt it would be permissible to serve me because I had been baptized in the Greek Orthodox church as a child.)

I didn't realize the Lord had something in store for me that night that would impact my life greatly.

All forty-nine nuns, along with my friends and me, went to the newly built prayer chapel. The nuns began worshipping the Lord, "singing in the Spirit" and blessing the Lord for about half an hour. The sisters gave several words of prophecy that encouraged me.

By then I was on my knees crying because I sensed such a tremendous presence of the Lord there.

It was an anointing that I had never before experienced in a communion service, not even in my own church. It was a divine, powerful presence of God that I can't describe except to say, "Jesus walked into that little room."

Just as they were finishing that time of worship, I began to feel a numbness in my arms and chest. I didn't know that the mother general had just gone to the table and picked up the communion wafer. Now she began to speak the words of the apostle Paul from 1 Corinthians 11:23:

> For I received from the Lord that which I also delivered to you: that the Lord Jesus on the same night in which He was betrayed took bread....

As I was kneeling and praising the Lord with my hands extended directly in front of me, the mother general put the wafer in my mouth.

At that moment I felt a fire literally go through me, and as that took place something else amazing happened. I sensed on the tips of my fingers something like a robe — a soft, silky fabric.

I thought maybe I was touching one of the sister's robes or that my mind was playing tricks on me. I wasn't sure what it was. So I opened my eyes to see whether someone had stepped in front of me. There was no one.

I wanted to make sure it wasn't just my mind, so I closed my eyes again. By this time, of course, I was weeping and trembling. Again I felt the robe. I thought, This can't be. I opened my eyes. Nothing was there.

I closed my eyes again, and there it was. I could still feel it. So I moved my hands closer toward each other. Then I was stopped. I could not move them any closer. I felt a physical body there.

I believe I was literally kneeling at the feet of Jesus.

After that communion service, I couldn't quit singing. That whole night I felt as if I were floating. I went back to my hotel room and asked the Lord, "What happened to me?" The Lord began to open my understanding about the subject of communion.

Whenever we have communion, we are having communion with the Lord. When we celebrate the Lord's supper, He Himself comes.

I want to share with you what the Lord showed me through that experience and as I studied the Word. In 1 Corinthians 10:16, the Bible says:

> The cup of blessing which we bless, is it not the communion of the blood of Christ? The bread which we break, is it not the communion of the body of Christ?

This verse says, "There is communion in the communion." Often when we take communion, we don't realize that we are to have communion with the Lord Himself. It's not just a practice because of tradition or what we were told by our fathers or our mothers. Yes, it's a remembrance of what He did for us two thousand years ago at Calvary. But at the same time, it is a communion with Him in the present! He comes today to fellowship with you as a son or as a daughter.

Even though I'd been a Christian and a preacher for many years, it was not until that night at the convent that I began to see something new in the communion. The fact is, when we have communion, Jesus wants to come and have fellowship with us as we partake of "the Lord's supper."

We call it the Lord's supper because it's His supper, not ours.

I don't mean to suggest, of course, that people ought to expect to have the same experience I had. I believe the Lord revealed Himself that evening to me in that unusual way in order to teach me. Yet communion is always a time when the presence of the Lord can be very real to our spiritual senses.

Being Worthy

I was so thrilled by this new understanding about the Lord's supper that I wanted to do everything I could to keep the "communion in the communion." Paul's warning in the Scriptures became so real:

Therefore whoever eats this bread or drinks

this cup of the Lord in an unworthy manner will be guilty of the body and blood of the Lord (1 Cor. 11:27).

Why was he saying this to the Corinthian church? What would cause them to turn communion with the Lord into a vain ceremony? The apostle Paul gives us five reasons.

1. *There were divisions among them.* "For first of all, when ye come together in the church, I hear that there be divisions among you; and I partly believe it" (1 Cor. 11:18, KJV).

2. *There were heretical teachings in the church.* "For there must be also heresies among you, that they which are approved may be made manifest among you" (1 Cor. 11:19, KJV).

3. *We see selfishness in this church.* "For in eating every one taketh before other his own supper: and one is hungry, and another is drunken" (1 Cor. 11:21, KJV).

4. *They despised the house of God.* "What? have ye not houses to eat and to drink in? or despise ye the church of God..." (1 Cor. 11:22, KJV).

5. *They've become very proud and look down on others.* "...and shame them that have not?" (1 Cor. 11:22, KJV).

When Paul warned against celebrating the Lord's supper in an unworthy manner, he was talking about the sins in the Corinthian church. Some of their sins were even committed at the Lord's table!

Paul said that many of the Corinthians were "weak and sick," and some had even died because of their lack of discernment. That's a negative thing. But by the same token, if we partake worthily, I believe there will be health and strength, rather than weakness and sickness. Paul goes on to say:

> For if we would judge ourselves, we would not be judged. But when we are judged, we are chastened by the Lord, that we may not be condemned with the world (1 Cor. 11:31-32).

If we would judge ourselves, then God wouldn't have to judge us. But if He does judge, He is only doing it for the sake of your redemption. In Psalm 32 we see both kinds of judgment — how God judges man and how man can judge himself.

Listen to the way David describes himself when he "kept silent" — in other words, when he did not judge himself and confess his sin.

> When I kept silent, my bones grew old
> Through my groaning all the day long (v. 3).

Here we see that when he didn't confess his sin, his physical body was affected. Remember that Paul said, "For this reason [participating in communion unworthily] many are weak and sick among you" (1 Cor. 11:30).

God often judges us by withdrawing a sense of His presence from us. Living without the presence of the Lord is like the dryness of a summer without rain.

> For day and night thy hand was heavy upon me: my moisture is turned into the drought of summer (v. 4, KJV).

So how can we come back into the Lord's favor? David demonstrates what to do.

> I acknowledged my sin to You,
> And my iniquity I have not hidden.
> I said, "I will confess my transgressions to
>   the Lord,"
> And You forgave the iniquity of my sin (v.
>   5).

Speaking of David, the Lord said, "He is a man after My own heart" (see 1 Sam. 13:14). Why? Because David sought after the Lord.

When the prophet Samuel told Saul that God had rejected him, Saul asked Samuel for forgiveness (1 Sam. 15:25). When the prophet Nathan confronted David for stealing another man's wife, you don't find David saying, "Forgive me, Nathan" (see 2 Sam. 12). Rather he said, "Have mercy upon me, O God" (Ps. 51:1).

The big difference between David and Saul was this: Saul sought forgiveness; David sought the one who forgives.

David sought God and asked Him to forgive him. We also must confess our sins to the Lord. When we acknowledge our transgressions to Him, then the Bible says, "You forgave the iniquity of my sin" (Ps. 32:5).

Amazingly, the Bible calls those who confess their sins godly.

> For this cause everyone who is godly shall
>   pray to You
> In a time when You may be found (v. 6).

Look at how David's relationship with God changed after he confessed his sin. He wrote:

> You are my hiding place;
> You shall preserve me from trouble;
> You shall surround me with songs of deliverance (Ps. 32:7).

So we see the way God responds when we repent.

Paul states that we must judge ourselves before partaking of the Lord's supper. How do we judge ourselves? By confessing our sins. And what is the result? Communion with the Lord is restored.

What Do We Remember?

When Jesus was celebrating the first communion with His disciples, He told them, "Do this in remembrance of Me." What should we remember when we come to the Lord's table?

First, dear saint, I know you thank God that Jesus died in your place to free you from the consequences of your sins. But He did so many other things for you on the cross.

The Bible declares that Jesus suffered rejection and became acquainted with grief for you and me.

> He is despised and rejected by men,
> A Man of sorrows and acquainted with
>   grief (Is. 53:3).

On the cross Jesus bore our sins and the consequences of our sins.

> Surely He has borne our griefs
> And carried our sorrows (Is. 53:4).

The word *grief* here is the Hebrew *choliy* which means "weak, sick or afflicted." Surely He hath borne our weaknesses, sicknesses and afflictions. The Hebrew word for *sorrows* is *makob*, which means "pain or grief."

The Scriptures are clear: Jesus not only died to take away our sins; He died to take away our sicknesses. The New Testament confirms that fact in Matthew 8:16-17.

> When evening had come, they brought to Him many who were demon-possessed. And He cast out the spirits with a word, and healed all who were sick, that it might be fulfilled which was spoken by Isaiah the prophet, saying,
>
> > "He Himself took our infirmities
> > And bore our sicknesses."

Matthew was referring to Isaiah 53:4, which speaks of Christ being stricken, smitten and afflicted.

So Jesus died not only to take away your sins, but to take away your sicknesses.

I believe the psalmist was speaking prophetically of the benefits of the cross when he wrote Psalm 103.

> Bless the Lord, O my soul, and forget not
> all His benefits (v. 2).

Why shouldn't we forget His benefits? I believe when you forget what God has done for you, He is grieved. The psalmist said of the children of Israel:

> And again and again they tempted God,
> And pained the Holy One of Israel.
> They did not remember His power,
> The day when He redeemed them from the
> adversary (Ps. 78:41-42, NAS).

It's important to God that you remember what He has done for you. That's why we celebrate the Lord's supper — to remember all the good things He has done for us through the cross. And here they are in Psalm 103:

- "Who forgives all your iniquities" (v. 3). All your sins are washed; all your sins are forgiven. All you have to do is repent and receive Him as your Savior.

- "Who heals all your diseases" (v. 3). I'm so

glad the verse doesn't say, "Who forgave" and "who healed." It says, "Who forgives" — present tense — and "who heals" — present tense. He still forgives; He still heals.

- "Who redeems your life from destruction" (v. 4).

- "Who crowns you with lovingkindness and tender mercies" (v. 4).

- "Who satisfies your mouth with good things" (v. 5). The Bible says God satisfies you with good things. He never gives bad things; He always gives good things. As my friend Oral Roberts says, "God is a good God."

- "So that your youth is renewed like the eagle's" (v. 5). When we know His benefits, He'll renew us.

- "The Lord executes righteousness and justice for all who are oppressed" (v. 6). Because of the cross, we are defended from the oppressor.

I want to share with you one more benefit of the cross that the Lord showed me many years ago. It has blessed me greatly.

Come Into the Throne Room

Paul tells us in Philippians 2:5-8 something wonderful about what Jesus has done for us. He took seven "steps" to descend from His heavenly throne to the cross.

1. "Who, being in the form of God, did not consider it robbery to be equal with God" (v. 6),

2. "but made Himself of no reputation" (v. 7),

3. "taking the form of a bondservant" (v. 7),

4. "and coming in the likeness of men" (v. 7).

5. "And being found in appearance as a man" (v. 8),

6. "He humbled Himself" (v. 8)

7. "And became obedient to the point of death, even the death of the cross" (v. 8).

And, as we read in Philippians 2:9-11, God took seven "steps" to restore His throne to Him.

1. "Therefore God also has highly exalted Him" (v. 9)

2. "and given Him the name which is above every name" (v. 9),

3. "that at the name of Jesus every knee should bow" (v. 10),

4. "of those in heaven" (v. 10),

5. "and of those on earth" (v. 10),

6. "and of those under the earth" (v. 10),

7. "and that every tongue should confess that Jesus Christ is Lord, to the glory of God the Father" (v. 11).

Now in the book of Hebrews the Scripture declares that after the Lord Jesus purged our sins, He "sat down at the right hand of the Majesty on high" (Heb. 1:3). Sitting speaks of a finished work; the right hand speaks of power. Jesus received all authority and all power. "Majesty on high" speaks of His being the King of kings and Lord of lords.

Because He is on that throne, the Bible says we have "boldness to enter the Holiest by the blood of Jesus" (Heb. 10:19). Jesus went from the *throne to the cross* to save us. He went from the *cross to the throne* to become our high priest and enable us to enter God's presence.

Whenever you celebrate the Lord's supper, remember that it is because of the blood of Jesus Christ that we can have fellowship with God. And as we recall what He has done for us when His body was broken and His blood was shed, then the presence of God will descend.

I've seen in my own experience that through the blood of Jesus, the anointing of God always comes — not only on my private, personal prayer life, but even during church services and the great miracle services.

I never conduct a service without thanking Him for the blood. And every time I do, the presence of God descends, and miracles take place. In the old covenant, God responded with fire when blood was offered on the altar. So it is today. When the blood of Jesus is honored, when the cross is honored, the Holy Spirit comes and touches people's lives.

I pray that the presence of the Holy Spirit will become great in your life as a result of reading this book. And I pray your love for the Lord will increase until that glorious day when you see Him face to face.

Book Opening

1. R. A. Torrey, *How to Obtain Fullness of Power* (Tarrytown, N.Y.: Fleming H. Revell Company, 1897; Murfreesboro, Tenn.: Sword of the Lord Publishers, n.d.), p. 19.

Chapter 1

1. Maxwell Whyte, *The Power of the Blood* (Springdale, Pa.: Whitaker House, 1973), pp. 87-88, 90.
2. Ibid., p. 23.

Chapter 3

1. See *The Bethany Parallel Commentary* (Minneapolis, Minn.: Bethany House Publishers, 1985), comments from Jamieson, Fausset, Brown and Adam Clarke for Gen. 3:21.
2. H. Clay Trumbull, *The Blood Covenant* (Kirkwood, Mo.: Impact Books, 1975), pp. 18-20.

Chapter 6

1. Torrey, *Fullness of Power*, p. 60.
2. Ibid.
3. *The Best of E. M. Bounds on Prayer* (Grand Rapids, Mich.: Baker Book House, 1981), p. 27.

Chapter 7

1. David Alsobrook, *The Precious Blood* (Paducah, Ky.: David Alsobrook Ministries, 1977), pp. 50-58.
2. New Bible Dictionary, ed. J. D. Douglas (Wheaton, Ill.: Tyndale House, 1987), s.v. plants.

Chapter 8

1. Derek Prince, *The Spirit-Filled Believer's Handbook* (Orlando, Fla.: Creation House, 1993), p. 251.
2. Andrew Murray, *The Power of the Blood* (Fort Washington, Pa.: Christian Literature Crusade, 1984), p. 28.
3. Billy Graham, *Revival in Our Time* (Wheaton, Ill.: Van Kampen Press, 1950), p. 119.

Chapter 9

1. Alsobrook, *The Precious Blood*, pp. 60-68.
2. *The International Standard Bible Encyclopedia* (Grand Rapids, Mich.: Wm. B. Eerdmans Publishing Co., 1982), s.v. shoe; sandal by David M. Howard.

Chapter 10

1. Torrey, *Fullness of Power*, p. 23-24.
2. Ibid., p. 24.
3. From the song "There Is Power in the Blood," text and music by Lewis Jones.

Chapter 11

1. Murray, *The Power of the Blood*, p. 32-33.

Chapter 13

1. From the song "Praise My Soul, the King of Heaven," words by Henry F. Lyte, music by John Goss. Adapted from Psalm 103.

Chapter 14

1. A. W. Tozer, *The Pursuit of God* (Harrisburg, Pa.: Christian Publications, Inc., 1948), p. 11.

Chapter 15

1. From the song "Amazing Grace! How Sweet the Sound," text by John Newton.
2. Barbara Bowen, *Strange Scriptures That Perplex the Western Mind* (Grand Rapids, Mich.: Wm. B. Eerdmans Publishing Co., 1985), p. 36.